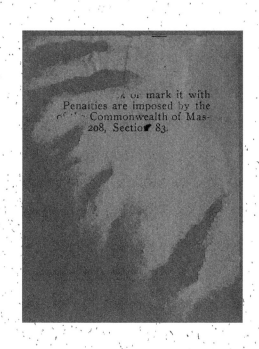

GENEALOGY

—of—

WILLIAM SANFORD

—of—

MADISON, N. Y.

HEMAN H. SANFORD
See No. 1097.

*4434.153

SANFORD

GENEALOGY

THE BRANCH OF

WILLIAM OF MADISON, N. Y.

——OF THE——

SIXTH AMERICAN GENERATION.

——BY——

HEMAN HOWES SANFORD,

SYRACUSE, N. Y.

1894.

Heman H. Sanford —
May 1, 1894.

PREFATORY.

N. B.—For convenience of reference a number has been assigned to each member of the family. Figures in ( ) indicate the American generation, reckoning as first, John the immigrant of A. D., 1631.

C. stands for child or children, b. for born, m. married, and d. died. The P. O. address is under the name. To trace from individuals to their families, find their number on the left hand margin, then turn on till the same number is found again in the middle of a page. To trace backward reverse the process.

The central person of these records is William (6), No. 50. Those who precede are simply to show his ancestry, and following him is as full a record of his descendants as I have been able to obtain. I take pleasure in acknowledging my special obligations, for assistance in the early records, to Hon. Wm. P. Sheffield of Newport, R. I., and in later records to each of those who have acted as secretaries for the families to which they belong.

Notwithstanding all the care and painstaking correspondence, I am well aware that many errors and omissions will be found. In this respect I wish to ask a special favor, which I trust that no member of our family will be unwilling to grant, that is, if there is positive proof of any error or omission, that it be reported to me or to my son Wm. John, as soon as possible ; and, if reference is made to any one in these records, that care be taken to give the number with the name. I would further request that any changes in P. O. address, and every birth, marriage and death, with the *time* and *place*, be reported at once, that at some future time a more complete edition may be issued. I would also recommend that this branch of the Sanford family continue the custom of appointing a registrar to whom all these reports shall be made, and that a corrected edition be issued, once in about twenty-five years.

Two extra copies of the present edition will be mailed to any address upon the receipt of one dollar.

HEMAN H. SANFORD,
Ostrom Ave., Syracuse, N. Y.

HISTORICAL.

About the middle of August, 1631, John, the son of Samuel and Elleanor Sanford, of Alford, Lincolnshire, England, sailed for America, in the ship Lyon, Captain Pierce, in company with John Eliot the missionary to the Indians, John Winthrop Jr., afterwards governor of Ct., and others. They arrived out of Boston harbor, on Nov. 3d, and after two days landed in the new world.   A few items from the colonial records will be of interest to his descendants.

Before the close of the year he was recorded as a church member. Aug. 6, '33, he was chosen to oversee the building of cart bridges over Stony and Muddy rivers.   May 14, '34, appointed to examine the condition of the ordnance, powder and shot.

Sept. 3, '34, he was chosen cannoneer for the Port of Boston, and for two years service already rendered at said Port, and for one year to come he was allowed £20. Sept. 8, '36, he was allowed £10 for service the year past.   Oct. 28, '36, again appointed cannoneer and surveyor of the arms and ammunition, salary £30 for himself and man.   Nov. 2, '37, discharged and allowed £13, 6 s., 8 d., for the year past.

Nov. 20, '37, he and others were ordered to deliver up all guns, pistols, swords, powder, shot, etc., because "The opinions and revelations of Mr. Wheelwright and Mrs. Hutchinson have seduced and led into dangerous errors many of the people here in New England."   Being allowed to leave the colony they went to Portsmouth, R. I., where on March 7, 1638, he and eighteen others signed the following compact : "We, whose names are underwritten, do hereby solemnly, in the presence of Jehovah, incorporate ourselves into a Bodie Politick, and, as he shall help, will submit our persons, lives and estates unto our Lord Jesus Christ, the King of Kings and Lord of Lords, and to all those perfect and most absolute laws of his, given us in his holy word of truth, to be guided and judged thereby."

May 13, '38, at a general meeting of the inhabitants, it was ordered that the meeting house should be set on the neck of land that goes over to the main island, where he and John Coggeshall shall lay it out.   May 20, '38, he had six acres allotted him north of the great cove.

June 27, '38, he and four others were appointed to repair highways. 1640, constable ; Mar. 16, '41, Freeman ; '44, Lieutenant ; '47-'49, assistant; '53, President of Portsmouth and Newport.

His will was dated June 22, 1653,—proved in the same year. His wife Bridget was exx., and the overseers, Brother-in-law Edward Hutchinson of

Boston, and friends Richard Tew of Newport, Richard Borden, Philip Sherman and Edward Fisher of Portsmouth, and his son John Sanford.

"To my wife my new dwelling house, in which I live, with all and every chamber and room therein, and half of the cook room, all my right in the great orchard, land on the north side of new dwelling house, meadow and a third of all cattle and movables, for life. To son John certain land and the ferry, the old house, half the cook room, and two houses on the south side of a certain path, all to him and his heirs male, failing of which, testator's son Samuel shall have, and so on. To John also great roan mare, besides one of his own, a negro man and wife, four oxen, two cows, the great ferry-boat, five ewes and five ewe lambs and a sow, a feather bed, cutlass, great fowling piece, etc. To son Samuel forty acres of land at Black Point, four oxen, two cows, brown mare, five ewes, five ewe lambs, a sow, a Spanish gun, sword, belt, best cloak and hat, feather bed and great Bible. To son Peleg, at age, twenty acres at Black Point, second roan mare, five ewes, five ewe lambs, two cows, a sow, French gun, a sword, etc. To Restcome, at age, forty acres at Black Point and like legacies to sons Wm., Ezbon and Elisha. To daughter Eliphal £100, of which £60 to be hers at marriage and £40 at her mother's marriage or death. To daughter Annie £60 at marriage. To sons Samuel, Peleg, Restcome, William, Ezbon and Elisha rest of the estate. The hay and corn on the ground for cattle and family. And I do bequeath my children unto my wife, next unto God, entreating that they may be carefully provided for and tenderly brought up as hitherto they have been, and that they may be well educated and brought up in the fear of the Lord. To overseers a ewe lamb. Inventory £824 11s. 1d. viz : 60 pounds gunpowder, £94 10s.; 84 lbs. shot, £1 1s.; 8 pairs men's shoes and a pair of women's shoes, £1 16s.; 18 trading hatchets, peage £58 10s., (8 per penny), carpet, cupboard, cloth, stuff cloak, long cushion, corselet wanting the gorget, seven chairs, table, form, cradle, books £2. Five pewter platters and flaggon, two silver spoons, six old scythes, warming-pan, three fowling pieces, cutlass, three old swords, flock bed for the negroes, 80 ewe sheep, £120 ; 36 wethers, 9 of them rams, £27 ; 4 old oxen, £30 ; 8 young oxen, £56 ; 6 steers, 2 bulls, 4 calves, 12 cows, 4 heifers, 7 yearlings, 5 calves, bay horse, foal, 4 mares, ten sows, five hogs, two negroes and a negro boy, £62 10s.; great ferry boat and tackling, £20 ; canoe £10, hay and corn £40.

Nov. 20, 1653, his widow took receipts of John and Samuel for legacies.

Oct. 17, 1663, his widow, now wife of Wm. Phillips of Boston, took receipt of Bartho Stratton, husband of her daughter Eliphal for legacy. June 17, 1670 she took receipt from son Ezbon for his share of the estate. Her will was dated Sept. 29, 1696. Proved Aug. 18, 1698. Exrs. daughter Eliphal Stratton and sons Samuel, and Wm. Phillips. In this she makes bequests to the above children and to son Peleg Sanford, to grandson Wm. Stratton, to daughters Sarah and Deborah Phillips, and to granddaughter in England, daughter of son Esbon, to Elizabeth, wife of grandson Wm.

Stratton, to children of her three sons and daughter, to granddaughter Ann Atkins, and her daughter Ann, and her daughter Eliphal, to granddaughter Bridget Ladd and her daughter Bridget, to grandson Wm. Stratton's daughter Bridget and great grandson Edward Ladd.

Of John Sanford (2), the son, we have these records : Freeman, May 17, 1653; General Treasurer 1655-'64, Commissioner 1656-'63, General Recorder 16 years between 1656-'76, Attorney General '63, '64, '70, '71 ; Deputy 16 years between '64 and '86, Assistant '64, '65 and '80. Aug. 10, '67, he enlisted a troop of horse.

May 7, '73, on Committees to treat with the Indian Sachems ; Apr. 4, '76, he and three others appointed to take the census of R. I., and on committee to have care of a barrel of powder for Portsmouth, and see that two guns now in yard of Wm. Brenton, deceased, be placed in Portsmouth, one on Ferry neck, and the other near the house of John Borden. Oct. 31, '77, he and 47 others were granted 5,000 acres, to be called East Greenwich. Dec 22, '86, apprized of his appointment by Sir Edmond Andros as member of his council.

Samuel (3) son of John (2) is found living at Tiverton, and mentioned as a weaver. His will was made Dec. 27, 1737, and proved and recorded at Taunton, Mass., Sept. 19th, 1738. He gave his real estate to his sons to be divided by themselves. To his daughters Mrs. Mary Taber and Mrs. Eliphal Hart, he gave £15 each—probably besides dowry at marriage. The sons being unable to agree the division was given to arbitrators, one of whom is mentioned as their uncle John Manchester, Tiverton. Restcome, the oldest, received his share adjacent to and parallel with the Dartmouth town line, and his brothers westerly from him. From the description—see deeds, Liber 27, p. 487 Taunton—Samuel had a large estate.

Restcome (4), oldest son of Samuel (3) was Justice of the Peace and Town Clerk of Tiverton in 1768.

William (5) son of Restcome (4) was a house carpenter. He purchased land in Tiverton, where he was living, of Elijah Allen, Jan. 4, 1782 ; recorded at Taunton, Liber 60, p. 447.

William (6) son of William (5) lived in Tiverton about a mile north of "The Head of the River," afterwards called Adamsville. The house was on rising ground west of the road. From the top of a large rock S. W. of the house the sea or river could be seen. He removed with his family about May, 1797, to New York State. They came up the Mohawk by scow boats pushed by setting poles. From Utica they went with teams to the old farm which had first been taken up by Thomas Brownell Simmons, though squatters had made two small clearings, one of which was called Teller's chopping. Captain Niles had been on a farm farther north a year or two. They built a log house on the east side of the present road and in about one year they moved into a house of split basswood logs on the low hill at the south east. The present framed house was built about 1806.

7

The nearest village was the "Indian Opening" west of Madison village. A great part of the county was called Hamilton and the towns were called by number, 1st, 2d, etc. When they were named, Hamilton was given to the 4th, also called Payne Settlement. From the old home the children have scattered over the United States as the following records will show.

Samuel and Elléanor Sanford, of Alford, Lincolnshire, Eng., were the parents of.

1 JOHN SANFORD, who m. 2 Elizabeth Webb.
                    m.^{2} 3 Bridget Hutchinson, dr. of Susanna.
                    He died, Portsmouth, R. I., 1653, and Bridget
                    d. 1698.

(2) C. of 1 and 2.

4	JOHN SANFORD,		b. Boston, Mass., June 4, 1632.
			d. E. Greenwich, R. I., 1687.
5	Samuel	"	b. Boston, Mass., July 14, 1634.
			d. Portsmouth, R. I., Mar. 18, 1713.

(2) C. of 1 and 3.

6	Eliphal	"	b. Boston, Mass., Dec. 9, 1637.
			d. Jan. 18, 1724.
7	Peleg	"	b. Portsmouth, May 10, 1639.
			d. Newport, R, I., 1701.
8	Endcome	"	b. Portsmouth, Feb. 23, 1640 ; d. young.
9	Restcome	"	b. Portsmouth, Jan. 29, 1642.
			d. unmarried, 1637.
10	William	"	b. Portsmouth, Mar. 4, 1644 ; d. unmarried.
11	Esbon	"	b. Portsmouth, Jan. 25, 1646.
12	Frances	"	b. Portsmouth, Jan. 9, 1648 ; d. young.
13	Elisha	"	b. Portsmouth, Dec. 28, 1650. Living in 1676.
14	Anne	"	b. Portsmouth, Mar. 12, 1652.
			d. Boston, Aug. 26, 1654.

4 JOHN SANFORD, m. 15 Elizabeth Spatchurst, dr. of Henry of Ber-
                  muda, Aug. 8, 1654 ; d. Dec. 6, 1661.
               m.^{2} 16 Mary Greene, (wid. of Peter, and dr.
                  of Samuel Gorton) Apr. 17, 1663 ; d. 1688.

(3) C. of 4 and 15.

17	Elizabeth Sanford,		b. Portsmouth, (?) July 11, 1655.
18	Mary	"	b.	"	Aug. 18, 1656.
19	Susanna	"	b.	"	July 31, 1658.
20	Rebecca	"	b.	"	June 23, 1660.

8

(3) C. of 4 and 16.

21	Mary	"	b. Portsmouth,		Mar. 3, 1664.
22	Eliphal	"	b.	"	Feb. 20, 1666.
23	John	"	b.	"	June 18, 1672.
24	SAMUEL	"	b.	"	Oct. 5, 1677.

24 SAMUEL SANFORD, m. 25 Deborah, dr. of Wm Manchester.

(4) C. of 24 and 25.

26	RESTCOME SANFORD,		b. Tiverton, R. I.,		July 27, 1704.
27	Peleg	"	b.	"	"	Mar. 8, 1708.
28	Mary	"	b.	"	"	May 7, 1710.
29	Eliphal	"	b.	"	"	May 12, 1714.
30	Samuel	"	b.	"	"	Nov. 21, 1716.

26 RESTCOME SANFORD, m. 31 Elizabeth Lake, Dec. 9, 1724.
m.[2] 32 Content ———

(5) C. of 26 and 31.

33	WILLIAM SANFORD,		b. Tiverton, R. I.,		June 17, 1725.
34	Restcome	"	b.	"	"	June 18, 1727.
35	Abigail	"	b.	"	"	Feb. 19, 1729.
36	David	"	b.	"	"	Sept. 28, 1730.
37	Peleg	"	b.	"	"	Jan. 24, 1733.
38	Mary	"	b.	"	"	Sept. 24, 1735.
39	Samuel	"	b.	"	"	Oct. 11, 1737.
40	Deborah	"	b.	"	"	Dec. 23, 1739.
41	Sarah	"	b.	"	"	Nov. 7, 1741.

(5) C. of 26 and 32.

42	Elizabeth	"	b.	"	"	Feb. 18, 1748.
43	George	"	b.	"	"	Oct. 18, 1750.
44	Ephraim	"	b.	"	"	May 28, 1752.

33 WILLIAM SANFORD, m. 45 Mary Waight.

(6) C. of 33 and 45.

46	Joseph Sanford,		b. Tiverton, R. I.,		June 15, 1746.
47	Abigail	"	b.	"	"	Nov. 28, 1748.
48	Peleg	"	b.	"	"	Oct. 23, 1751.
49	Eliphal	"	b.	"	"	Apr. 22, 1755.
50	WILLIAM	"	b.	"	"	Sept. 27, 1757.
			d. Madison, N. Y., Oct. 26, 1837.
51	Thomas	"	b. Tiverton, R. I., June 30, 1761.

ABRAHAM SANFORD
See No. 61.—Age 98, May 5, 1894.

50 WILLIAM SANFORD, m. 52 Abigail Simmons, R. I., 1780.

                 b. R. I., Oct. 31, 1760.

                 d. Madison, N. Y., Sept. 26, 1819.

                 m.[2] 53 Susan Brigham (Howe), Madison, N.Y., 1824.

                 d. Madison, N. Y., 1845.

(7) C. of 50 and 52.

54	Asa Sanford,	b. Tiverton, R. I., Sept. 24, 1781.
		d. Madison, N. Y., Nov. 5, 1873.
55	Prudence "	b. Tiverton, R. I., Sept. 10, 1783.
		d. Madison, N. Y., Dec. 20, 1858.
56	Priscilla "	b. Tiverton, R. I., Oct, 17, 1785.
		d. Tiverton, R. I., Aug. (?) 1786.
57	Mary "	b. Tiverton, R. I., May 14, 1787.
		d. Madison, N. Y., Mar. 22. 1829.
58	William Hicks Sanford,	b. Tiverton, R. I., Nov. 22, 1789.
		d. Conneaut, Asht'a Co., Ohio, Sept. 7, 1874.
59	Peleg Sanford,	b. Tiverton, R. I., Feb. 21, 1792.
		d. Clark Co., Ill., Mar. 20, 1848.
60	Nancy "	b. Tiverton, R. I., Mar. 9, 1794,
		d. Windham, Portage Co., Ohio, Oct. 8, 1882.
61	Abraham ."	b. Tiverton, R. I., May 5, 1796.
	Ostrom Av., Syracuse, N. Y.	
62	Lucretia Sanford,	b. Madison, N. Y., Mar. 2, 1802.
		d. Darwin, Clark Co., Ill.

---

54 Asa Sanford, m. 63 Edith Simmons, Madison, N. Y., Oct. 15, 1805.

                 b. Aug. 11, 1788, d. Madison, Oct. 14, 1835.

(8) C. of 54 and 63.

64	A son	b. Madison, N. Y., Aug. 16, 1806.
		d. " " Aug. 31, 1806.
65	Phebe Sanford,	b. Georgetown, N. Y., Aug. 9, 1808.
		d. Madison, N. Y., Apr. 8, 1829.
66	Priscilla "	b. Georgetown, N. Y., June 1, 1810.
		d. Madison, N. Y., Apr. 9, 1829.
67	Asa Brownell Sanford,	b. Georgetown, N. Y., July 21, 1812.
	York, Michigan.	
68	Susan Sanford,	b. Madison, N. Y., Sept. 1, 1814.
		d. " " June 4, 1831.
69	Bradford Pierce Sanford, b.	" " Jan. 9, 1817.
	Fulton, N. Y.	

70 Harriot Maria Sanford, b. Madison, N. Y., June 27, 1819.
                                         d.   "   "   Sept. 15, 1874.
71 Thomas Simmons   "   b.   "   "   Dec. 18, 1821.
                                           d. Ann Arbor, Mich., Mar. 31, 1888.
72 Oliver Hazard Perry "   b. Madison, N. Y., Dec. 30, 1824.
    Bouckville, N. Y.
73 George Damon Sanford, b.   " ·   "   June 10, 1831.
    York, Mich.

---

67 Asa B. Sanford, m. 74, Cynthia Warren, Nov. 13, 1833.
                           b. Dec. 1, 1813.

(9) C. of 67 and 74.

75 Harriet Priscilla Sanford, b. York, Mich., June 16, 1835.
                                 d.   "   "   May 28, 1843.
76 Julius Franklin   "   b.   "   "   Aug. 3, 1837.
    Saline, Mich.
77 Mary Maria   "   b.   "   "   Oct. 18, 1839.
                                 d. Saline, Mich., Jan. 4, 1866.
78 Helen Elizabeth   "   b. York, Mich., Mar. 10, 1842.
                                 d.   "   "   Oct. 30, 1876.
79 Aaron Warren   "   b.   "   "   May 21, 1845.
    York, Mich.
80 Orson Riley   "   b.   "   "   July 27, 1847.
    Wolverine, Mich.
81 George Elmer   "   b.   "   "   Aug. 20, 1851.
    York, Mich.
82 Eva Ardella   "   b.   "   "   Jan. 12, 1854.
    New Castle, Placer Co., Cal.
83 Edith Sanford,   b.   "   "   July 6, 1859.
    Virginia City, Nev.

---

76 Julius F. Sanford, m. 84, Lydia Antoinette Silsbury, Jan. 2, 1859.
                            : b. Aug. 14, 1839.

(10) C. of 76 and 84.

85 Herbert Lester Sanford, b. York, Mich., Feb. 13, 1860.
86 Clarence Leslie   "   b.   "   "   Aug. 15, 1861.
    611 Francis St., Jackson, Mich.
87 Lydia Antoinette Sanford, b. York, Mich., Aug. 5, 1869.

---

86 Clarence L. Sanford, m. 87[2] Ella Bertha Bauer, Aug. 23, 1893.
                             b. Jackson, Mich., Feb. 5, 1869.
77 Mary M. Sanford. m. 88 Harley Marvin Russell, Oct. 18, 1859.
                           b. May 21, 1819.

(10) C. of 77 and 88.

89 Edward Everett Russell, b. Saline township, Mich., Aug. 12, 1861.
Saline, Mich.
90 Frederick L. " b. " " " Mar. 27, 1865.

89 Edward E. Russell, m. 91 Nellie Tucker, Saline, May 17, 1893.
                                b. Chelsea, Mich., May 26, 1871.
79 Aaron W. Sanford, m. 92 Emma Melissa Tuttle, Dec. 23, 1866.
                                b. June 4, 1849.

(10) C. of 79 and 92.

93 Willis Warren Sanford, b. York, Mich., Oct. 25, 1867.
94 Otis Apollos " b. " " Nov. 20, 1873.
95 Mary Emma " b. " " Dec. 23, 1878.

93 Willis W. Sanford, m. 96 Bertha Ann Craig, June 18, 1890.
                                b. Jan. 2, 1869.

(11) C. of 93 and 96.

97 Thurlow Sanford, b. York, Mich., Nov. 24, 1891.
98 Fauntleroy Raymond Sanford, b. " " Dec. 3, 1892.

80 Orson R. Sanford, m. 99 Mary Elizabeth Hinkley, Sept. 20, 1869.
                                b. York, Mich., June 20, 1846.
                                d. " " Apr. 16, 1885.
                        m.[2] 99[2] Mrs. Luella Chandler Colescott,
                                Cheboygan, Mich., Sept. 21, 1893.
                                b. Kokomo, Ind., June 12, 1860.

(10) C. of 80 and 99.

100 Lena Sanford, b. Saline, Mich., Nov. 2, 1871.

81 George E. Sanford, M. D., m. 101 Mary M. Royall, Feb. 21, 1875.
                                b. Feb. 19, 1851, d. March 17, 1875.
                        m.[2] 102 Emma Jane Robinson, Mar. 6, 1876.
                                b. Sept. 16, 1852.

(10) C. of 81 and 102.

103 Asa Milton Sanford, b. York, Mich., Oct. 6, 1877.
104 Christine " b. Genoa, N. Y., Dec. 25, 1880.
                                d. Dec. 25, 1880.
105 Inez Emma " b. Eaton, N. Y., June 16, 1882.
                                d. " " Apr. 12, 1883.
106 Rose " b. " " Apr. 3, 1884.

107	Thomas S. Sanford,		b. Eaton, N. Y., Mar. 26, 1885.
			d. " " Apr. 10, 1885.
108	George Oliver	"	b. York, Mich., Dec., 29, 1886.
109	Lilly	"	b. " " Jan. 27, 1889.
110	John	"	b. " " Mar. 12, 1890.
			d. " " Aug. 5, 1890.
111	Lawrence	"	b. " " July 28, 1891.
112		"	b. " " May 29, 1893.
112²	Max	"	b. " " May 29, 1893.
			d. " " Oct. 1, 1893.

82 Eva A. Sanford, m. 113 George W. Harris, Ann Arbor, Nov. 11, 1874.
                b. Mt. Pleasant, N. Y., Oct. 11, 1852.
                Divorced, Auburn, Cal., Jan. 12, 1883.
                d. LaCentre, Wash., Sept. 6, 1884.
         m.² 114 Jonathan Ashbell Robinson, Feb. 26, 1883.
                b. Copley Center, O., Feb. 21, 1834.

(10) C. of 82 and 113.

115	Lizzie Ardella Harris,	b. Mt. Pleasant, N. Y., Sept. 29, 1875.
116	Thomas Stephen "	b. Williams, Colusa Co., Cal., July 14, 1879.
		d. Sacramento, Cal., Jan. 20, 1881.

(10) C. of 82 and 114.

117 Sarah Shirley Robinson, b. New Castle, Cal., Sept. 21, 1886.

83 Edith Sanford, m. 118 Charles Adin Cook, Dec. 24, 1876.
                b. Sept. 5, 1856. Divorced.
         m.² 119 James Singleton, P. O., Virginia City, Nev.
                b. Aug. 1833. Divorced.
         m.³ 120 Rowland Howard Cutts, Virginia City, Nev.,
                May 12, 1893.

(10) C. of 83 and 118.

121	Cynthia Janette Cook,	b. Oct. 27, 1877.
	Jack Pine, Crawford Co., Mich.	
122	George Cook,	b. July 17, 1879.
123	Nettie "	b. Oct. 9, 1880.

69 Bradford P. Sanford, m. 124 Lavinia Gage Peckham, Jan. 1, 1840.
                b. Hamilton, N. Y., May 9, 1818.
                d. Jan. 8, 1879.
         m² 125 Emeline Wright, Nov. 22, 1879.
                b. Volney, Mar. 22, 1822 ; d. Aug. 25, 1887.
         m.³ 126 Cerelia E. Ward, Feb. 1, 1888.
                b. Valley Mills, N. Y., June 26, 1840.

13

(9) C. of 69 and 124.

127 Cornelia Priscilla Sanford, b. Madison, N. Y., July 5, 1841.
    Mt. Pleasant, N. Y.
128 Oliver Peckham Sanford, b. Volney, N. Y., July 6, 1846.
                    d.   "   "   Dec. 3, 1847.
129 Henry Llewelyn   " b.   "   "   June 29, 1853.
    Fulton, N. Y.
130 Asa Bradford   " b.   "   "   Oct. 25, 1885.
    South Scriba, N. Y.

---

127 Cornelia P. Sanford, m. 131 Abram H. Lewis, Jan. 12, 1857.
                    b. Volney, N. Y., July 28, 1831.

(10) C. of 127 and 131.

132 Elpha Betsey Lewis, b. Volney, N. Y., Mar. 1, 1859.
    Oswego, N. Y.
133 Henry Abram   " b.   "   "   Dec. 4, 1864.
    South Scriba, N. Y.
134 Hattie Lavinia Lewis, b.   "   "   Dec. 25, 1866.
                    d.   "   "   Feb. 21, 1872.
135 Mina Lucinda   " b.   "   "   Feb. 4, 1871.
    South Scriba, N. Y.
136 Arthur Charles Lewis, b.   "   "   Aug. 9, 1880.
    South Scriba, N. Y.

---

132 Elpha B. Lewis, m. 137 George Delos Dexter, Apr. 2, 1879.
                    b. Palermo, N. Y., May 27, 1857.

(11) C. of 132 and 137.

138 Earnest Wiliam Dexter, b. Volney, N. Y., Jan. 9, 1882.
                    d.   "   "   Aug. 9, 1882.
139 Earl James   " b.   "   "   Apr. 30, 1884.
138 Glen George   " b. Oswego, N. Y., May 21, 1893.
    Oswego, N. Y.

---

133 Henry A. Lewis, m. 140 Ada Emeline Manwarren, March 3, 1891.
                    b. Red Creek, N. Y. Aug. 8, 1869.

(11) C. of 133 and 140.

141 Mabel Emigene Lewis, b. Volney, N. Y., Mar. 28, 1892.

---

135 Mina L. Lewis, m. 142 John C. Smith, March 4, 1891.
                    b. Palermo, March 29, 1865.

(11) C. of 135 and 142.

143 Lewis Bradford Smith,   b. S. Scriba, March 13, 1892.

---

129 Henry L. Sanford, m. 144 Rhoda A. Ives, Dec. 7, 1875.
    b. Sept. 22, 1855 ; d. Volney. July 14, 1888.
    m.[2] 145 Annie Belle DeMott, March 12, 1890.
    b. Niles, Mich., Apr. 27. 1860.

(10) C. of 129 and 144.

146 Vyron Spencer Sanford, b. Volney, N. Y., June 18, 1878.
    d.   "   "   Mar. 28, 1881.
147 Minnie Rebecca   "   b.   "   "   July 17, 1880.
148 John Bradford   "   b.   "   "   Sept. 9, 1983.
149 Floyd Albern   "   b.   "   "   July 23, 1886.
150 Earl   "   b.   "   "   July 6, 1888.
    d.   "   "   July 20, 1888.

(10) C. of 129 and 145.

151 Lizzie Catharine Sanford, b. Mt. Pleasant, Dec. 29, 1891.

---

130 Asa B. Sanford, m. 152 Mary Jane Ward, Feb. 13, 1877.
    b. Volney, N. Y., Nov. 28, 1860.

(10) C. of 130 and 152.

153 Emigene Lavinia Sanford, b. Volney, N. Y., May 4, 1880.
154 Elmer Pierce   "   b.   "   "   Nov. 7, 1883.
    d.   "   "   Nov. 16, 1883.
155 Ernest P.   "   b.   "   "   May 14, 1886.
    d.   "   "   May 13, 1887.
156 Erwin Asa   "   b.   "   "   July 19, 1889.
South Scriba, N. Y.

---

70 Harriet M. Sanford, m. 157 Sidney Tompkins, Apr. 10, 1855.
    b. Madison, N. Y.

---

71 Thomas S. Sanford, m. 158 Elpha L. Lowry, Sept. 20, 1846.
    They had a daughter who lived 3 or 4 months.

---

72 Oliver H. P. Sanford, m. 159 Fanny Blair Tompkins, March 19, 1856.
    b. Oct. 14, 1832.

(9) C. of 72 and 159.

160　Henry William Sanford, b. Madison township, N. Y., Dec. 19, 1857.
　　　Avon, Fulton Co., Ill.
161　Hattie Phebe Sanford, b. " " " Sept. 20, 1859.
　　　Bouckville, N. Y.
162　Fannie Matilda Sanford, b. " " " June 18, 1862.
　　　Lebanon, N. Y.
163　Charles Brownell " b. " " " June 19, 1865.
　　　Morrisville, N. Y.
164　Samuel Stephen " b. " " " Apr. 12, 1867.
　　　Bouckville, N. Y.
165　Albert Gilbert " b. " " " May 29, 1875.
　　　Hamilton, N. Y.

160　Henry W. Sanford, m. 166 Jennie S. Dunnahugh, Greenbush, Ill.,
　　　　　　　　　　　　　March 29, 1882.
　　　　　　　　　　　　b. Augusta Co., Va., Feb. 6, 1859.

(10) C. of 160 and 166.

167　Albert Sanford, b. Avon, Ill., Aug. 11, 1883.
168　Alta " b. " " Aug. 11, 1883.
169　Gilbert Lester Sanford, b. " " Feb. 5. 1886.
170　Fannie Ethel " b. " " June 29, 1889.
171　Clarence Brownell " b. " " Nov. 14, 1891.
　　　Avon, Ill.

162　Fannie M. Sanford, m. 172 Arthur Stephen Lindsay, Feb. 20, 1890.
　　　　　　　　　　　　b. Sept. 8, 1864.

73　George D. Sanford, m. 173 Electa Wilmot, Oct. 14, 1856.
　　　　　　　　　　　　b. Florence, N. Y., Feb. 16, 1833.

(9) C. of 73 and 173.

174　Harriet Alzina Sanford, b. Lodi, Mich., July 28, 1862.
　　　Saline, Mich.
175　Sidney Wilmot " b. " " May 26, 1864.
　　　York, Mich.
176　William Clyde " b. " " Jan. 21, 1869.
　　　York, Mich.
177　Charles Thomas " b. " " Oct. 30, 1870.
　　　York, Mich.
178　Minnie Rosalie " b. " " Sept. 10, 1873.
　　　Milan, Mich.

174 Harriet A. Sanford, m. 179, George Frederick Marken, Ann Arbor,
Apr. 10, 1884.
b. York, Apr. 7, 1860.

(10) C. of 174 and 179.

180	Clyde Marken,		b. York, Mich., Aug. 26, 1885.
181	Earl	"	b. Saline, " July 30, 1889.

---

175 Sidney W. Sanford, m. 182, m. Florence Lovica Montanye, Ann Arbor, April 24, 1889.
b. Leslie, Mich., Jan. 9, 1868.

(10) C. of 175 and 182.

183	Ray William Sanford,		b. York. Mich., July 17, 1890.
184	Hazel	"	b. " " Dec. 3, 1891.
184²	Ferris Glen,	"	b. " " Aug. 11, 1893.

---

178 Minnie R. Sanford, m. 185 Wila Pomeroy Lamkin, York, Apr. 5, 1893.
b. Raisinville, Mich., Aug. 4, 1861.

---

55 Prudence Sanford, m. 186 Charles Peckham, Madison, Dec. 20, 1798.
b. Tiverton, R. I., Sept. 20, 1775.
d. Madison township, Mar. 14, 1859.

(8) C. of 55 and 186.

187	Abigail Peckham,		b. Madison, N. Y., Jan. 29, 1800.
			d. " " Mar. 19, 1853.
188	Otis	"	b. " " Dec. 20, 1801.
			d. " " Oct. 30, 1802.
189	Orson	"	b. " " Jan. 11, 1803.
			d. " " May 23, 1886.
190	Ira	"	b. " " Sept. 20, 1805.
			d. " " July 16, 1873.
191	Jerusha	"	b. " " Nov. 12, 1806.
			d. " " May 6, 1892.
192	Lydia	"	b. " " Sept. 5, 1888.
			d. " " Apr. 1, 1889.
193	Mace Solsville, N. Y.	"	b. " " May 29, 1811.
194	Susanna	"	b. " " Nov. 9, 1812.
			d. " " June 25, 1890.
195	Sanford Solsville, N. Y.	"	b. " " Dec. 5, 1814.

17

196	Emily Peckham,		b. Madison, N. Y., Jan. 5, 1817.
			d. " " Jan. 12, 1858.
197	Nancy	"	b. " " Oct. 27, 1818.
			d. " " Oct. 30, 1818.
198	Sardis	"	b. " " Jan. 4, 1820.
			d. " " May 7, 1845.
199	Lucretia	"	b. " " Apr. 10, 1822.
			d. Hamilton, " July 28, 1862.
200	Wesley	"	b. Madison, N. Y., June 11, 1825.
			d. in infancy.
201	Priscilla	"	b. Madison, N. Y., June 19, 1827.
			d. " " June 20, 1888.
202	Mary	"	d. in infancy.

187 Abigail Peckham, m. 203 Curtiss Bacon, Madison, Nov. 8, 1823.

(9) C. of 187 and 203.

204	Lucetta Bacon,		b. Madison, July 27, 1824.
205	Harriet	"	b. " Feb. 13, 1827.
206	Mary	"	b. " Aug. 19, 1828.
207	Martha	"	b. " Oct. 25, 1829.
208	Julia Ann	"	b. " 1835.
209	Prudence	"	b. " Mar. 1, 1840 ; d. Aug. 1881.
210	Henry	"	b. " Dec. 29, 1842.

204 Lucetta Bacon, m. 211 John Carter, Madison, Oct. 13, 1843.
b. England, Oct. 1800.

(10) C. of 204 and 211.

212	Jeanette Carter, Madison, N. Y.	b. Madison, N. Y., July 25, 1843.
213	Harriet Carter, Madison, N. Y.	b. " " Jan. 22, 1845.
214	Ellen Carter, Madison, N. Y.	b. " " Oct. 10, 1847.
215	Mary Carter, Madison, N. Y.	b. " " May 3, 1849.
216	Stillman Carter,	b. " " Sept. 23, 1854.
		d. " " Feb. 14, 1863.

212 Jeanette Carter, m. 217 Randolph Briggs, Sept, 25, 1861.
b. 1838.

(11) C. of 212 and 217.

218	Letta Briggs,	b. Nov. 25, 1862.

218 Letta Briggs, m. 219 Will Benjamin, Mar. 24, 1886.
b. May 3, 1859.

(12) **C. of 218 and 219.**

220 Densie Benjamin, b. April 13, 1887.

---

213 Harriet Carter, m. 221 Millo Camp, 1866 ; b. 1847.

(11) **C. of 213 and 221.**

222 Cora Camp, b. July 3, 1869.

---

222 Cora Camp, m. 223 Edward Wells, Madison, June 10, 1891.
b. June 11, 1865.

(12) **C. of 222 and 223.**

224 Ethel Wells, b. Mar. 21, 1893.

---

214 Ellen Carter, m. 225 Chauncey Adams, Nov. 10, 1882.
b. June 24, 1827.

---

215 Mary Carter, m. 226 Addison Stevens, Madison, Jan. 14, 1871 ; b. 1841.

(11) **C. of 215 and 226.**

227 Lottie Stevens, b. Apr. 23, 1885 ; d. Jan. 8, 1889.

---

205 Harriet Bacon, m. 228 Jonathan Hazzard, July 25, 1852.
b. Feb. 13, 1827.

(10) **C. of 205 and 228.**

229 Robert Fulton Hazzard, b. Madison, Sept. 20, 1854.
230 Russell F. Hazzard, b. " Oct. 8, 1858.
231 Benjamin F. " b. " July 31, 1860.
232 Emogene " b. " Mar. 7, 1862.
233 Oliver Perry " b. " June 18, 1865.

---

225 Robert F. Hazzard, m. 234 Miranda Hart, Oct. 4, 1876.

(11) **C. of 229 and 234.**

235 Minnie May Hazzard, b. Madison, Sept. 11, 1877.

---

230 Russell F. Hazzard, m. 236 Ella Sayer, Nov. 20, 1890.

(11) C. of 230 and 236.

237 Genevieve Hazard, b. Sept. 26, 1891.

---

231 B. F. Hazzard, m. 238 Carrie Ward, Dec. 24, 1887.

(11) C. of 231 and 238.

239 Benjamin F. Hazzard, b. Dec. 14, 1890; d. July 10, 1891.

---

232 Emogene Hazzard, m. 240 Calvin Sigsbee, Dec. 15, 1880.

(11) C. of 232 and 240.

241 Pearl J. Sigsbee, b. March 20, 1882.
242 Jason M.   "   b. May 30, 1893.

---

206 Mary Bacon, m. 243 T. W. Collins, 1848 ; b. Aug. 19, 1828.

(10) C. of 206 and 243.

244 DeWayne Collins,   b. Jan. 9, 1849 ; d. June 8, 1849.
245 Albert   "   b. Feb. 8, 1850 ; d. July 23, 1861.
246 Lucina   "   b. July 19, 1852.
247 Almira   "   b. July 3, 1854 ; d. Aug. 2, 1861.
248 Thomas   "   b. Sept. 10, 1863 ; d. Sept. 11, 1863.
249 Willim W.   "   b. Feb. 3, 1864 ; d. July 18, 1865.
250 Minnie   "   b. Jan. 27, 1868 ; d. April 30, 1871.
251 William H. "   b. March 19, 1870.

---

246 Lucina Collins, m. 252 W. H. Myers, 1875.

(11) C. of 246 and 252.

253 Willie Myers, b. July 7, 1876.

---

207 Martha Bacon, m. 254 Fred. Bacon Nov. 20, 1849.
                         b. Aug. 9, 1828.

(10) C. of 207 and 254.

255 LaFayette Bacon,   b. Madison, Feb. 2, 1850 ; d. June 16, 1854.
256 Rosalette   "   b.   "   Nov. 20, 1852.
257 Emeline   "   b.   "   April 1, 1855.
258 LaFayette   "   b.   "   April 27, 1857.
259 Adelbert   "   b.   "   Nov. 13, 1873.

---

256 Rosalette Bacon, m. 260 Irving Baker, Nov. 15, 1872.

(11) C. of 256 and 260.

261 Frederick B. Baker, b. Nov. 17, 1873.
362 Eva B.   "   b. Jan. 29, 1877.

---

257 Emeline Bacon, m. 263 George Scott, Hamilton, Dec. 25, 1873.
b. Aug. 13, 1845.

(11) C. of 257 and 263.

264	Annie E. Scott,	b. Nov. 20, 1874.
265	Emma A. "	b. Oct. 18, 1876.
266	Adah A. "	b. July 14, 1878.
267	Walter P. "	b. Nov. 2, 1882.
268	Abbie "	b. July 17, 1885.
269	Wallace "	b. Feb. 25, 1889.

---

259 Adelbert Bacon, m. 270 Alta Bacon, March 7, 1893.
b. Nov. 13, 1873.

---

208 Julia Ann Bacon, m. 271 Clark Bacon, 1848; b. 1828.

(10) C. of 208 and 271.

272	DeElton Bacon,	b. Madison, 1850 ; d. 1852.		
273	DeElton "	b.	" .	1853.
274	Dellephene "	b.	"	1855.
275	Duane "	b.	"	1857.
276	Jerome "	b.	"	1860.

---

273 DeElton Bacon, m. 277 Louise Skinner, Hamilton, 1878.

---

274 Dellephene Bacon, m. 278 David Bemis, Hamilton, 1881.

(11) C. of 274 and 278.

279 George Bemis, b. 1885.

---

209 Prudence Bacon, m. 280 George Smith, March 1, 1857.

(10) C. of 209 and 280.

281	Abbie A. Smith, Hubbardsville, N. Y.	b. March 14, 1858.
282	Newton W. Smith, Baldwinsville, N. Y.	b. Dec. 8, 1859.
283	George H. Smith, Poolville, N. Y.	b. Oct. 13, 1862.

21

282 Newton W. Smith, m. 284 Lottie McHuron, Sept. 12, 1888.

283 George H. Smith, m. 285 Annie Weeks, March 21, 1892.

210 Henry Bacon, m. 286 Lillie F. Bacon, Mar. 16, 1871 ; d. Apr. 11, 1886.
　　　　　　　m.² 287 Sarah Hughes, Nov. 3, 1887.

(10) C. of 210 and 286.

288 Dean W. Bacon,　　　　b. Madison, Oct. 16, 1871.
289 LeRoy O. "　　　　　b. " July 12, 1875.

(10) C. of 210 and 287.

290, 291 Twin boys,　　　　b. and d. March 17, 1890.
292 Lottie M. Bacon,　　　b. June 10, 1891.

288 Dean W. Bacon, m. 293 Dora Lloyd, Jan 29, 1891.

189 Orson Peckham, m. 294 Delia Thompson, Aug. 28, 1825.
　　　　　　　　　b. July 15, 1803 ; d. Jan. 29, 1877.
　　　　　　　m.² 294² Mrs. Abigail Bigelow, June, 1877.
　　　　　　　　　b. Ct., Jan. 16, 1806.

(9) C. of 189 and 294.

295	Jason Peckham, Scriba, N. Y.	b. Madison township, N. Y., Sept. 7, 1826.			
296	Ruth Peckham,	b.	"	"	" March 4, 1831.
		d.	"	"	" April 6, 1837.
297	Eli "	b.	"	"	" July 31, 1833.
		d.	"	"	" June 9, 1838.
298	Jeanette " Arenac, Mich.	b.	"	"	" Nov. 17, 1836.
299	Jerusha Peckham,	b.	"	"	" Nov. 17, 1836.
		d.	"	"	" March 7, 1839.
300	Maria "	b.	"	"	" March 18, 1839.
		d.	"	"	" July 10, 1851.

295 Jason Peckham, m. 301 Imogene Lewis, Solsville, Jan. 23, 1859.
　　　　　　　　b. Solsville, Nov. 24, 1827.
　　　　　　　　d. Madison, March 25, 1870.
　　　　　　m.² 302 Alice Fish, Scriba, N. Y., Sept. 5, 1871.
　　　　　　　　b. Scriba, August 4, 1846.

22

(10) C. of 295 and 301.

303 Belle Alice Peckham, b. Madison, N. Y., Feb. 6, 1861.
Scriba, N. Y.
304 Delia Atlanta " b. " " May 29, 1863.
Scriba, N. Y.

(10) C. of 295 and 302.

305 Edith Peckham. b. Scriba, N. Y., Oct. 6, 1873.
306 Orson " b. " " June 2, 1877.

---

304 Delia A. Peckham, m. 307 George Kocher, Oswego, Dec. 10, 1890.
b. Oswego, Sept. 19, 1866.

(11) C. of 304 and 307.

308 Mable Alice Kocher, b. Scriba, N. Y., April 18, 1892.
309 Carl " b. " " March 6, 1893.

---

298 Jeanette Peckham, m. 310 Charles Kilmer, Sept. 15, 1857.
b. Madison Co., N. Y., Nov. 1, 1833.

(10) C. of 298 and 310.

311 Orson Kilmer, b. Madison, N. Y., Feb. 15; 1861.
Arinac, Mich.
312 Carrie Kilmer, b. Scriba, N. Y., Dec. 27, 1867.
d. " " March 1, 1870.
313 Lillian " b. " " July 11, 1874.
d. " " Aug. 15, 1874.

---

311 Orson Kilmer, m. 314 Harriet Shaw, March, 1879.
b. Feb. 15, 1863.

(11) C. of 311 and 314.

315 Carrie Kilmer, b. Arenac, Mich., April 27, 1880.
316 Delia " b. " " July 7, 1881.

---

190 Ira Peckham, m. 317 Phebe Simmons, Madison, N. Y., April 7, 1831.
b. Sept. 5, 1812 ; Madison tp., Jan. 16, 1883.

(9) C. of 190 and 317.

318 Wesley Peckham, b. Madison, N. Y., Sept. 10, 1832.
d. " " Oct. 15, 1837.
319 Morris " b. " " Sept. 2, 1834.
d. " " July 8, 1837.
320 Lewis W. " b. " " Oct. 30, 1836.
Bouckville, N. Y.

321	Mary A. Peckham,		b. Madison, N. Y.,	Apr. 13, 1839.
			d. " "	June 30, 1842.
322	Samuel	"	b. " "	June 14, 1842.
			d. " "	Oct. 11, 1844.
323	Eliza	"	b. " "	May 30, 1844.
			d. " "	March 5, 1847.
324	Mary Ann	"	b. " "	Feb. 26, 1846.
			d. " "	Dec. 20, 1847.
325	Infant,		b. " "	Dec. 31, 1849 ; d. ——
326	Sidney,	"	b. " "	Sept. 18, 1851.
			d. " "	Jan. 12, 1888.

320　Lewis W. Peckham, m. 327 Mary Crandall, May 1, 1860.
　　　　　　　　　　　b. June 29, 1839.

(10)　C. of 320 and 327.

328	Ettie J. Peckham,		b. Madison, N. Y.,	March 24, 1861.
329	Daisy	"	b. " "	June 19, 1867.
330	Jennie E.	"	b. " "	July 23, 1869.
331	Lewis W.	"	b. " "	June 20, 1873.
			d. " '	March 24, 1889.
332	R. Earl	"	b. " "	Feb. 8, 1878.

191　Jerusha Peckham, m. 333 Cyrus Thompson, Madison, Aug. 28, 1825.
　　　　　　　　　　　b. March 19, 1797 ; d. April 5, 1867.

(9)　C. of 191 and 333.

334	Emily Thompson,		b. Madison, N. Y.,	Oct. 4, 1831.
			d. " "	July 5, 1858,
335	Delia	"	b. " "	Aug. 13, 1835.
			d. " "	Nov. 6, 1874.
336	Alfred	"	b. " "	Aug. 22, 1837.
	Madison, N. Y.			

334　Emily Thompson, m. 337 John Vicory, March 22, 1854 ; b. 1828.

(10)　C. of 334 and 337.

338	Charles Vicory,	b. April 3, 1856.
	Hamilton, N. Y.	

338　Charles Vicory, m. 339 Jennie Chandler, Oct. 15, 1878.
　　　　　　　　　　　b. July 9, 1864.

(11) C. of 338 and 339.

340	Floyd C. Vicory,	b. April 9, 1880.
341	Ernest "	b. Nov. 28, 1883.
342	Madge "	b. May 13, 1887.
343	Earl "	b. Feb. 16, 1889.
344	Mabel J. "	b. Aug. 30, 1891.
	Hamilton, N. Y.	

335 Delia Thompson, m. 345 Brewer Risley, Feb. 23, 1859.
b. July 6, 1832.

(10) C. of 335 and 345.

346 Emma Risley,   b. Aug. 23, 1868.

346 Emma Risley, m. 347 Rev. John Carson Long, Hamilton, May 13, 1891.
b. Alexandria, Va., Oct. 2, 1866.

336 Alfred Thompson, m. 348, Mary Ann Risley, Dec. 18, 1861.
b. April 13, 1842 ; d. Dec. 25, 1893.

192 Lydia Peckham, m. 349 Abel Rundell.
b. March 27, 1802 ; d. Oct. 11. 1880.

(9) C. of 192 and 349.

350	Myra Rundell,	b. Madison, N. Y., Aug. 22, 1831.			
351	Calista "	b.	"	"	Jan. 1834 ; d. May 25, 1868.
352	Prudence "	b.	"	"	Nov. 25, 1836.
	Hamilton, N. Y.				
353	George Rundell,	b.	"	"	July 10, 1837.
354	Cyrus "	b.	"	"	Feb. 20, 1839; d. Mar. 21, 1836.
355	Helen "	b.	"	"	Dec. 12, 1843 ; d. Sep. 29, 1882.
356	Roselet "	b.	"	"	1844 ; d. Mar. 27, 1856.
357	Eugenia "	b.	"	"	Nov. 28, 1848.
	Pratts Hollow, N. Y.				
358	William Rundell,	b.	"	"	Oct. 3, 1852 ; d. Apr. 3, 1854.

350 Myra Rundell, m. 359 Henry Whitman, Jan. 1, 1855.
b. Knoxboro, Sept. 15, 1832.

(10) C. of 350 and 359.

360	W. Burr Whitman,	b. July 20, 1858.
361	Albert T. "	b. Sept. 18, 1860.
362	May "	b. Aug. 8, 1868.
	Pratts Hollow, N. Y.	

362　May Whitman, m. 363 James Fagan, March 4, 1891.
　　　　　　　　　　　b. Sandy Creek, Del. Co., Jan. 22, 1868.

(11) C. of 362 and 363.

364　Maude Alice Fagan,　　b. June 2, 1892.

353　George Rundell, m. 365 Phœbe Rice, July 24, 1861.
　　　　　　　　　　　b. Sept. 16, 1838 ; d. Sept. 11, 1891.

(10) C. of 353 and 365.

366　David Rundell,　　　b. Feb. 28, 1862.
367　Anna　　"　　　　b. May 10, 1864.
　　　Peterboro, N. Y.

366　David Rundell, m. 368 Anna Brown, Hamilton, Nov. 4, 1882.
　　　　　　　　　　　b. Cazenovia, N. Y., April 8, 1864.

(11) C. of 366 and 368.

369　Burton Rundell,　　　b. June 27, 1883.
370　Beatrice　　"　　　b. May 12, 1889.

367　Anna Rundell, m. 371 Dennis Pope, Hamilton, May 26, 1884.
　　　　　　　　　　　b. North Bay, July 14, 1855.

(11) C. of 367 and 371.

372　Nellie Pope,　　　　b. Feb. 20, 1889.
373　Infant son,　　　　b. Sept. 1, 1891 ; d. Sept. 10, 1891.

354　Cyrus Rundell, m. 374, Sophronia Fairchild, Hamilton, Feb. 14, 1860.
　　　　　　　　　　　b. Augusta, Dec. 17, 1841.

(10) C. of 354 and 374.

375　William C. Rundell,　b. Oct. 7, 1863 ; d. Oct. 21, 1863.
376　Nellie　　"　　　b. Feb. 1, 1866.
377　Edith　　"　　　b. Aug. 3, 1880.
　　　Hamilton, N. Y.

376　Nellie Rundell, m. 378 Frederick Nicholson, April 17, 1886.
　　　　　　　　　　　b. March 4, 1861.

(11) C. of 376 and 378.

379　Arthur Nicholson,　　b. Aug. 22, 1888.

355　Helen Rundell, m. 380 John Constantine, Madison, Nov. 16, 1869.
　　　　　　　　　　　b. Ireland, April 17, 1831.

(10) C. of 355 and 380.

381 Lena Constantine,   b. May 4, 1873.
382 Herbert   "   b. April 5, 1874.
383 Jerome   "   b. Sept. 22, 1877.

---

193 Mace Peckham, m. 384 Mary Tabor, Cazenovia, July 9, 1832.
                b. Cazenovia, May 11, 1811 ; d. Mar. 1842.
          m.² 385 Lucy Ann Rice, Waterville, N.Y., Oct. 27, 1843.
                b. Madison, Dec. 10, 1821.

(9) C. of 193 and 384.

386 Flora Peckham,   b. Solsville, N. Y., Feb. 2, 1838.
387 Adelaide "   b.   "   " Oct. 25, 1841 ; d. Aug. 26, 1859.

(9) C. of 193 and 385.

388 Augustus Peckham, b. Solsville, N. Y., Aug. 7, 1848.
389 Sardis   "   b.   "   " Mar. 23, 1854.
390 Anna   "   b.   "   " June 5, 1861.
391 U. Grant,   "   b.   "   " Mar. 6, 1864.
    Solsville, N. Y.

---

386 Flora Peckham, m. 392 Adelbert Lyon, Augusta, N. Y., July 9, 1861.
                b. Madison, Feb. 25, 1842 ; d. June 15, 1885.

(10) C. of 386 and 392.

393 George Lyon,   b. Solsville, N. Y , Aug. 27, 1864.
394 Warren "   b.   "   " Feb. 16, 1870.
395 Grace   "   b.   "   " Sept. 12, 1876.
    Solsville, N. Y.

---

393 George Lyon, m. 396 Mary Kneeland, Augusta, Oct. 23, 1889.
                b. Augusta, Jan. 27, 1860.

(11) C. of 393 and 396.

397 Estella Lyon,   b. April 10, 1891.

---

394 Warren Lyon, m. 398 Gertrude Basher, June 29, 1890.
                b. Augusta, N. Y., Jan. 27, 1859.

---

388 Augustus Peckham, m. 399 Ida Sheldon, Solsville, Aug. 7, 1869.
                b. Solsville, April 27, 1832.

(10) C. of 388 and 399.

400	Burt Peckham,	b. Solsville, Sept. 6, 1873.
401	William "	b. " Oct. 30, 1877.
402	Harry "	b. " Aug. 12, 1890.

389 Sardis Peckham, m. 403 Lydia Sayer, Augusta, Dec. 7, 1881.
b. Morris, Sept. 9, 1860.

(10) · C. of 389 and 403.

| 404 | Glenn Peckham, | b. Augusta, N. Y., Jan. 29, 1883. |
| 405 | May " | b. Solsville, " Jan. 23, 1889. |

390 Anna Peckham, m. 406 Henry Beehler, Solsville, Oct. 25, 1881.
b. Oriskany Falls, Oct. 28, 1858.

391 U. Grant Peckham, m. 407 Bertha Basher, Solsville, Aug. 12, 1883.
b. Augusta, July 27, 1867.

(10) C. of 391 and 407.

408 Ella Peckham, b. Solsville, May 23, 1886.

194 Susanna Peckham, m. 409 John Johnson, Sept. 1, 1836.
b. Oct. 12, 1810; d. Jan. 21, 1891.

(9) C. of 194 and 409.

410	Isaac Johnson,	b. June 10, 1837.
411	Edward "	b. Sept. 16, 1842.
412	Myron "	b. May 27, 1847.
	Madison, N. Y.	

410 Isaac Johnson, m. 413 Martha Butchers, Nov. 4, 1857.
b. Nov. 19, 1834.

(10) C. of 410 and 413.

| 414 | Burt B. Johnson, | b. July 24, 1862. |
| 415 | W. Hollis " | b. May 5, 1866. |

414 Burt B. Johnson, m. 416 Martha Baker, Madison, June 11, 1889.
b. Madison, Jan. 21, 1868.

(11 C. of 414 and 416.

417 Clifford Baker Johnson, b. April 21, 1890.

415 W. Hollis Johnson, m. 418 Winona L. Taylor, April 8, 1890.
b. March 22, 1867.

(11) C. of 415 and 418.

419 Beryl Johnson,   b. Sept. 14, 1892.

---

411 Edward Johnson, m. 420 Frank Lewis, Dec. 24, 1862.
b. June 16, 1842.

(10) C. of 411 and 420.

421 Eva Johnson,   b. March 7, 1867.
422 Anna   "   b. Oct. 10, 1871 : d. Nov. 7, 1881.
423 Clarence "   b. May 8, 1876.

---

421 Eva Johnson, m. 424 George Brown.

---

412 Myron Johnson, m. 424² Alice Dann, Nov. 10, 1875.
b. June 17, 1853.

(10) C. of 412 and 424².

424³ Newell Johnson,   b. Madison, April 22, 1880.

---

195 Sanford Peckham, m. 424⁴ Amanda Lewis, Clinton, N.Y., Dec. 24,1845.
b. Solsville, N. Y., March 19, 1821.

(9) C. of 195 and 424⁴.

425 Eugenia Peckham,   b. Solsville, Dec. 14, 1847.
10 Jewett Place, Utica, N. Y.
426 Carrie Peckham,   b.   "   Sept. 23, 1857.
626 East Main St., Rochester, N. Y.

---

425 Eugenia Peckham, m. 427 Henry F. Miller, Oct. 31, 1867.
b. Jan. 18, 1845.

(10) C. of 425 and 427.

428 Frank Peckham Miller,   b. July 3, 1872.
429 Grace Lillian   "   b. Buffalo, N. Y., July 26, 1874.
430 Henry Bradley   "   b. Utica, N.Y.,Aug. 29,1880; d. Sep. 18,1880.
431 Bessie Amanda   "   b.   "   " Aug. 17, 1881.
10 Jewett Place, Utica, N. Y.

---

426 Carrie Peckham, m. 432 George Benton Watkins, Solsville, Mar. 10, '73.
b. Utica, N. Y., August 12, 1852.

(10) C. of 426 and 432.

433   Maud Irene Watkins,   b. Buffalo, N. Y., July 16, 1874.
434   Emma May   "   b. Rochester, N. Y., Aug. 15, 1877.
435   Carrie Eugenia "   b.   "   "   May 11, 1881.
     626 East Main St., Rochester, N. Y.

---

433   Maud I. Watkins, m. 436 Louis Sinclair Foulkes, Rochester, N. Y.,
                      Sept. 12, 1893.

---

196   Emily Peckham, m. 437 Pixley Curtiss, Madison. Oct. 1840.
                 b. Madison, Oct. 18, 1815 ; d. May 2, 1863.

(9) C. of 196 and 437.

438   Aristene Curtiss,   b. Solsville, Nov. 8, 1842 ; d. Sep. 28, 1868.
439   Ella   "   b.   "   Dec. 6, 1844.

---

488   Aristene Curtiss, m. 440 Joseph Cook, 1862.

(10) C. of 438 and 440.

441   Allie Cook,   b. Madison. March 8, 1865.
               d. Morrisville, Dec. 4, 1890.
442   James "   b.   "   April 9, 1866.
     111 W. Park St., Rome, N. Y.

---

441   Allie Cook, m. 443 Na. Mott Campbell, Solsville, May 16, 1888.
                b. Eaton, N. Y., June 16, 1863.

(11) C. of 441 and 443.

444   Aristene Campbell,   b. Eaton, N. Y., Oct. 31, 1889.
     Randallsville, N. Y.

---

439   Ella Curtiss, m. 445 Julius Palmer, Madison, Nov. 22, 1864.
                b. Oriskany Falls ; d. Feb. 8, 1872.
            m.² 446 Charles Lewis, Feb. 23, 1876.
                b. Madison, April 18, 1843.

(10) C. of 439 and 445.

447   Burt Palmer,   b. Madison, Oct. 26, 1868.
     Irvington, Iowa.

30

(10) C. of 439 and 446.

448   Harry Lewis,   b. Geneva, Ill., Jan. 6, 1878.
      Irvington, Iowa.
449   Ralph Lewis,   b.   "   "   May 28, 1886.
                              d. March 29, 1888.

---

199   Lucretia Peckham, m. 450 Henry Neff, Hamilton, March, 1842.
                            b. Homer, N. Y., June 24, 1819.
                            d. Nov. 18, 1877.

(9) C. of 199 and 450.

451   Adelbert Neff,   b. Munsville, N. Y., Feb. 7, 1840.
                            d. Sept. 21, 1888.
452   Addie Neff,   b. Solsville, Feb. 3, 1848.
      Hubbardsville, N. Y.
453   Charles Neff,   b.   "   June 4, 1850.
454   Samuel   "   b. Hamilton, Jan. 1863 ; d. Aug. 21, 1863.
455   Jay   "   b.   "   Mar. 4, 1855 ; d. Dec. 27, 1857.

---

451   Adelbert Neff m. 456 Josephine Sayles, Madison, Sept. 16, 1867.
                         b. Moravia, Aug, 8, 1844.

(10) C. of 451 and 456.

457   Jay Neff,   b. Sept. 21, 1870.
458   Harry Neff,   b. April 21, 1878.

---

452   Addie Neff, m. 459 James Baxter, Solsville, March 2, 1875.
                      b. Oct. 14, 1844.

(10) C. of 452 and 459.

460   Roy Baxter,   b. Solsville, Feb. 23, 1876.
461   Lucretia Baxter,   b. Madison, March 21, 1882.

---

201   Priscilla Peckham, m. 462 Stiles Curtiss, Oct. 11, 1848.
                     b. March 9, 1817.

(9) C. of 201 and 462.

463   Charles Thompson Curtiss, b. Madison tp., N. Y., Feb. 3, 1854.
        Solsville, N. Y.
464   Minnie Jane Curtiss,   b.   "   "   Oct. 3, 1859.
      Solsville, N. Y.

---

57   Mary Sanford m. 465 Ezekiel Simmons, Madison, N. Y., 1805.
                     b. Dec. 1782 ; d. Madison, Sept. 29, 1829.

31

(8) C. of 57 and 465.

466 Anthony Simmons, b. Madison, July 15, 1806.
 d. Battle Creek, (?) Michigan.
467 William " b. Madison, Aug. 2, 1808.
Mexico, Oswego Co., N. Y.
468 Zarah Simmons, b. " Aug. 18, 1810.
Hamilton, N. Y.
469 Phebe Simmons, b. " Sept. 5, 1812.
 d. Bouckville, N. Y., Jan. 16, 1883.

---

466 Anthony Simmons m. 470 ——— ———
 m.² 471 Amanda Benson.

---

467 William Simmons m. 472 Lucinda Peckham, Madison, 1831.
 b. Madison, July 15, 1810.
 d. Richland, N. Y., July 27, 1864.
 m.² 473 Harriet Janette Purington, Oct., 1864.
 b. Cicero, (?) Feb. 25, 1838.

(9) C. of 467 and 472.

474 Semantha Melissa Simmons, b. Volney, N. Y., Aug. 23, 1839.
 d. Dugway, Oswego Co., July 27, 1886.
475 Hiram Burdette " b. Volney, N. Y., Feb. 9, 1843.
208 Pharis St., Syracuse, N. Y.
476 Janette Amanda Simmons, b. " " April 7, 1851.
New York City.

(9) C. of 467 and 473.

477 George William Simmons, b. Volney, April 17, 1870.
Mexico, N. Y.

---

474 Samantha M. Simmons, m. 478 Peter Carr, Volney, Jan. 1, 1855.

(10) C. of 474 and 478.

479 Mary J. Carr, b. Richland, N. Y., Jan. 17, 1856.
 d. " " Feb. 2, 1884.
480 Harriet A. " b. " " July 31, 1857.
Albany, N. Y.
481 Martha L. Carr, b. " " July 25, 1860.

---

479 Mary J. Carr, m. 482 James I. Doney, March 15, 1876.

(11) C. of 479 and 482.

483 Blanche E. Doney, b. Nov. 15, 1877 ; d. Sept. 3, 1880.

---

480 Harriet A. Carr, m. 484 Lawson G. Calkins, Aug. 28, 1878.

(11) C. of 480 and 484.

485	L. Earl Calkins,	b.	Albany, N. Y., July 16, 1879.
486	Elton "	b.	" " July 27, 1887.

---

481 Martha L. Carr, m. 487 James I. Doney, Sept. 29, 1884.

(11) C. of 481 and 487.

488	Bessie E. Doney,	b.	Dugway, Sept. 3, 1885.
489	Madge E. "	b.	" April 18, 1890.

---

475 Hiram B. Simmons, m. 490 Sarah M. Gates, New Haven, N. Y., Feb.
13, 1886.
b. Oswego Co., Nov. 24, 1843.

(10) C. of 475 and 490.

491 Esther Lucinda Simmons, b. Scriba, N. Y., April 9, 1867.
229 Lake View Av., Syracuse, N. Y.
492 Nellie May Simmons,   b. Volney, N. Y., Sept. 4, 1868.
905 Willis Av., Syracuse, N. Y.
493 Clara Belle Simmons,   b. Scriba, N. Y., April 23, 1871.
713 Marcellus St., Syracuse, N. Y.
494 Nettie Elmira Simmons, b. Volney, N. Y., April 3, 1875.
495 Melvin Hiram   "   b.   "   "   Oct. 31, 1879.
496 William Lyman   "   b. Syracuse, N. Y., June 18, 1884.

---

491 Esther L. Simmons, m. 497 Elvin Johnson, Syracuse, July 22, 1886.
b. Onondaga Co., N. Y., Oct. 22, 1862.

---

492 Nellie May Simmons, m. 499 George Wershiner, Syracuse, July 1, 1890.
b. Syracuse, Sept. 11, 1868.

(11) C. of 492 and 499.

500	George J. Wershiner,	b.	Syracuse, April 25, 1892.
501	William Lyman "	b.	Syracuse, July 14, 1893.

---

493 Clara B. Simmons, m. 502 Allen Munro Watkins, Syr., Aug. 28, 1890.

(11) C. of 493 and 502.

503	Carrie Elizabeth Watkins, b.	Syracuse, May 28, 1891.
504	—— " b.	" Jan. 4, 1894.

33

476　Janette A. Simmons, m. 505 George Kirk Hall, Madison, Feb. 22, 1882.
b. Madison, April 6, 1862.

468　Zarah Simmons, m. 506 Rebecca Peckham, Madison, Mar. 15, 1831.
b. Madison, Apr. 3, 1812 ; d. June 9, 1873.
m.[2] 506[2] Mrs. Rhoda Clark ; d. Jan. 7, 1886.
m.[3] 506[3] Mrs. Emily Preston, March 3, 1892.

(9)　C. of 468 and 506.

507	Mary Janette Simmons,	b. Madison Co., N. Y.,	May 2, 1833.
		d.　"　"	May 18, 1890.
508	Martha Amelia　"	b.　"　"	Aug. 8, 1837.
	Fowlersville, Mich.		
509	Franklin Augustus "	b.　"　"	Sept. 5, 1842.
510	Frances Augusta　"	b.　"　"	Sept. 5, 1842.

507　Mary J. Simmons, m. 511 Geo. B. Woodman, Madison, Mar. 15, 1855.

(10)　C. of 507 and 511.

512	Jay Morren Woodman,	b. Madison, July 12, 1859.
513	Zarah Simmons　"	b.　"	Oct. 1, 1861.
514	Mary Janette　"	b.　"	July 28, 1867.
515	Seth Jipson　"	b.　"	Dec. 8, 1869.

512　Jay M. Woodman, m. 516 Francena Stowell, Oct. 5, 1881.
b. May 26, 1861.

(11)　C. of 512 and 516.

517	George Merton Woodman,	b. Madison, Nov. 18, 1882.
518	Alton Rae　"	b.　"	Mar. 8, 1886.
519	Enoch Earl　"	b.　"	July 10, 1889.

513　Zarah S. Woodman, m. 520 Hannah Morgan, Nov. 20, 1884.
b. Jan. 1, 1863.

(11)　C. of 513 and 520.

521	Clarence Leo Woodman,	b. Madison Co., N. Y.,	Apr. 29, 1886.
	Hamilton, N. Y.		
522	Lou Eliza Woodman,	b.　"　"	Jan. 30, 1888.
523	Aurelia Mary　"	b.　"　"	Nov. 23, 1889.

515　Seth J. Woodman, m. 524 Cornia Hyde Clark, Lebanon, Mar. 9, 1892.
b May 13, 1870.

34

508 Martha A. Simmons, m. 525 Lyman Stewart, Madison, Feb. 26, 1857.
b. Plymouth, Jan 18, 1835.

(10) C. of 508 and 525.

526 Allen Burdett Stewart,   b. Madison, June 14, 1859.
527 Byron Burdell   "   b. Handy, Mich., July 14, 1871.
528 Mary Adell   "   b.   "   "   Sept. 16, 1873.
529 Martha Arbell   "   b.   "·   "   Sept. 16, 1873.

---

526 Allen B. Stewart, m. 530 Clara Adell Dawley, Aug. 12, 1880.
b. Sept. 24, 1862.

(11) C. of 526 and 530.

531 Henry Allen Stewart,   b. Feb. 27, 1883.

---

509 Franklin A. Simmons, m. 532 Ada Merritt.

---

510 Frances A. Simmons, m. 533 Nelson Sutton.
S. Minneapolis, Minn.

---

58 William H. Sanford removed to Erie Co., Pa., about 1818; to Ashtabula Co., Ohio, Jan. 1868; to Conneaut village, March, 1871.
58 William H. Sanford, m. 534 Priscilla Sawdy, Madison Co., N. Y., 1809.
b. Sangerfield, N. Y., Jan, 19, 1792.
d. Erie Co., Pa., Nov. 18, 1826.
m.[2] 535 Patience Sawdy, (widow of Daniel Frasure) 1827.
b. Sangerfield, N. Y., April 15, 1794.
d. Ashtabula Co., Ohio, Aug. 10, 1870.

---

(8) C. of 58 and 534.

536 Emily Sanford,   b. Madison Co., N. Y., Apr. 22, 1810.
d. Sangerfield, N. Y., March 1, 1816.
537 Jahaziel   "   b. Madison Co., N. Y., May 8, 1812.
Elgin, Ill.
538 Rhoda   "   b.   "   "   April 13, 1814.
Royalton, Morrison Co., Minn.
539 Samuel Sanford,   b. Sangerfield, N. Y., Mar. 1, 1816.
Thompson, Geauga Co., Ohio.
540 Henrietta French Sanford, b. Erie Co., Pa., July 4, 1818.
Sunset, Kane Co., Ill.
541 Caroline Sanford,   b.   "   "   Oct. 1, 1820.
d. Ashtabula, Ohio, Apr. 3, 1886.

542 Nehemiah Sanford,   b. Erie Co., Pa., Aug. 12, 1822.
Sunset, Kane Co., Ill.
543 David Sanford,   b.   "   "   Aug. 12, 1822.
Lundy's Lane, Erie Co., Pa.
544 Sophia Sanford,   b.   "   "   Sept. 29, 1824.
Erie, Pa., 1719 Plum Street.
545 Elizabeth Sanford,   b. Elk Creek. Pa., Nov. 8, 1826.
Conneaut, Ohio.

(8) C. of 58 and 535.

546 Alvin Thayer Sanford,   b. Elk Creek, Pa., Aug. 12, 1828.
Conneaut, Ohio.
547 Hannah Sanford,   b.   "   "   Jan. 30, 1832.
Conneaut, Ohio.
548 Isaac Sanford,   b.   "   "   July 8, 1835.
Shelby, Oceana Co., Mich.

---

537 Jahaziel Sanford, m. 549 Cordelia DeWolf, Belvidere, Ill.,May 28, 1852.
                 b. Springfield, Pa., July 12, 1832.
                 d. Dec. 7, 1878.

---

(9) C. of 537, and 549.

550 Polly Priscilla Sanford,   b. Gratiot, Lafayette Co.,Wis., June 2, 1855.
Elgin, Ill.
551 William Joseph "   b. Muscoda, Grant Co., Wis., May 22, 1858.
Rock Island Arsenal, Ill.
552 Ernest Alphonso Sanford, b. Stark, Vernon Co. Wis., Oct. 19, 1862.
Rock Island Arsenal, Ill.
553 Cordelia Eveline Sanford, b.   "   "   "   Sept. 11, 1865.
Elgin, Ill.
554 James Henry " b.   "   "   "   Apr. 29, 1867.
Rock Island Arsenal, Ill.

---

550 Polly P. Sanford, m. 555 William H. Goodwin, Sept. 1878.
                 b. August 1851.

---

552 Ernest A. Sanford, m. 556 Minnie Sweeney, Oct. 9, 1887.
                 b. Oct. 6, 1873 ; d. April 14, 1890.

---

(10) C. of 552 and 556.

557 Minnie Sanford,   b. Sept. 7, 1888.

---

553 Cordelia Eveline Sanford, m. 558 Edwin Nutt, Aug. 22, 1889.
b. July 13, 1865.

---

538 Rhoda Sanford, m. 559 James Sawdy, Elk Creek, Pa., Nov. 1832.
b. Romulus, N. Y., March 9, 1812.
d. Buckman, Minn., May 17, 1892.

---

(9) C. of 538 and 559.

560 Alexander Sawdy,   b. Lockport, Erie Co., Pa., May 12, 1835.
d. Gettysburg, Pa., July 27, 1863.
561 Caroline M.   "   b. Little Hope, Ohio, June 13, 1837.
d. Wattsburg, Pa., Sept. 1859.
562 Alonzo Perry "   b. Lockport, Pa., April 7, 1842.
Royalton, Minn.
563 James K. Polk Sawdy, b.   "   "   Nov. 12, 1845.
Ashtabula, O., (12 Centre Street).
564 Florence Amelia Sawdy, b.   "   "   Feb. 26, 1849.
Rice's, Benton Co., Minn.
565 George Harvey Sawdy, b.   "   "   Feb. 26, 1851,
Miles Grove, Erie Co., Pa.

---

560 Alexander Sawdy, m. 566 Julia Marie Carr, W. Springfield, Pa.,
June 27, 1858.
b. Conneaut tp., Erie Co., Pa., Aug. 22, 1838.

(10) C. of 560 and 566.

567 Walter Wilbur Sawdy,   b. Conneaut tp., Erie Co., Pa., Aug. 18, 1859.
315 W. 20th St., Erie, Pa.
568 Wilson Jerome Sawdy, b.   "   "   "   Nov. 23, 1862.
354 W. 18th St., Erie, Pa.

---

567 Walter W. Sawdy, m. 569 Justina M. Rapp, Sharpsville, Pa., Dec.
25, 1883.
b. Oakland, Mercer Co., Pa., Apr. 13, 1864.

(11) C. of 567 and 569.

570 Edith Frances Sawdy, b. N. Clarendon, Warren Co., Pa., Jan. 2, '85.
571 Wallace Albert   "   b. Cross', Erie Co., Pa., Feb. 16, 1889.

---

568 Wilson J. Sawdy, m. 572 Maud Belle Montgomery, Sharpsville, Pa.,
April 1, 1888.
b. Sharpsville, Pa., May 11, 1867.

(11) C. of 568 and 572.

573 Jennie Belle Sawdy,   b. Girard, Erie Co., Pa., Sept. 7, 1884.
574 Homer Robart "   b. Sharpsville, Pa., July 1, 1887.
                          d.   "   "   July 13, 1887.
575 Ella Frances   "   b. Girard, Erie Co., Pa., Feb. 19, 1890.

---

561 Caroline M. Sawdy, m. 576 Conley Casper Rouse, Lockport, Pa.,
                          Dec. 1856.
                          b. Wattsburg, Erie Co., Pa., June 21, 1831;
                          P. O., Union City, Erie Co., Pa.

(10) C. of 561 and 576.

577 Evaline Maria Rouse,   b. Wayne tp., near Wattsburg, Pa., Oct.
                          13, 1857.

---

577 Evaline M. Rouse, m. 578 Devillo Belmer Hitchcock, Union tp., Pa.,
                          Feb. 24, 1881.
                          b. Wattsburg, Pa., Dec. 25, 1855.

(11) C. of 577 and 578.

579 Belmer Devillo Hitchcock, b. Wattsburg, Amity tp., Erie Co., Pa.,
                          Oct. 18, 1882.
580 Stephen Conley   "   b. Union tp., Erie Co., Pa., Sept. 16, 1884.
581 Ward Park   "   b.   "   "   "   Aug. 26, 1885.
582 Grace Caroline,   "   b.   "   "   "   March 1, 1891.
583 Ford Jefferson   "   b. Union City,   "   "   June 17, 1893.

---

562 Alonzo P. Sawdy, m. 584 Amanda Dirr, Pittsburg, Pa., Sept. 22, 1864.
                          b. Minersville, Pa., March 27, 1846.

(10) C. of 562 and 584.

585 Luella Matilda Sawdy,   b. Lockport, Pa., March 23, 1867.
     Royalton, Minn.
586 Geo. Daniel Forrest "   b Girard, Pa., Nov. 16, 1868.
     Royalton, Minn.
587 James Hallock   "   b.   "   "   Apr. 15, 1870.
                          d. Buckman, Minn., Mar. 8, 1889.
588 Rhoda Leah   "   b. Girard, Pa., June 15, 1871.
     Chicago, Ill.
589 Urilda   "   b.   "   "   Oct. 2, 1873.
     Royalton, Minn.
590 Florence Gertrude "   b.   "   "   Dec. 19, 1875.
     Little Falls, Minn.

591	Royal Victor Swady,	b. Morrill, Minn., Jan. 15, 1878.
592	Arthur Garfield "	b. " " July 6, 1880.
593	Mary Edith "	b. " " July 22, 1883.
594	Ida Lucy "	b. " " Aug. 25, 1885.
595	Viola Vivian Faith "	b. Buckman, Minn., Apr. 2, 1891.
	Royalton, Minn.	

585 Luella M. Sawdy, m. 596 John Francis Hunter, Morrill, Minn., May 22, 1881.
b. Crawford Co., Pa., Sept. 20, 1852.

(11) C. of 585 and 596.

597	Charles Perry Hunter,	b. Morrill, Minn., July 16, 1882.
598	Asa Drake "	b. " " Jan. 16, 1884.
599	Abigail Jessie "	b. " " June 25, 1885.
600	Royal Vance "	b. " " Mar. 9, 1888.
601	Maud "	b. " " Apr. 1, 1891.

588 Rhoda L. Sawdy, m. 602 Harry Lawrence Smith, Chicago, Ill., Mar. 21, 1892.

589 Urilda Sawdy, m. 603 Jonathan Harry Kinney, M. D., Buckman, Minn., Sept. 8, 1891.
b. Ft. Ripley, Minn., April 29, 1853.

(11) C. of 589 and 603.

604 Alonzo Newcomb Kinney, b. Royalton, Minn., Sept. 13, 1892.

590 Florence G. Sawdy, m. 605 Abner Jesse Gorst, Royalton, Minn., Oct. 3, 1892.
b. Oak Ridge, Minn., March 12, 1870.

(11) C. of 590 and 605.

605[2] Walter Clayton Gorst, b. Little Falls, Minn., Sept. 3, 1893.

563 James K. P. Sawdy, m. 606 Eliza Hewitt, Fairview, Pa., July 12, 1868.
b. Keepville, Pa., 1847, divorced Mar. 28, 1873.
m.[2] 607 Mattie Miranda Potter, Conewago, Pa., Apr. 19, 1874.
b. Steamburg, Pa., Sept. 15, 1850.

(10) C. of 563 and 606.

| 608 | Fred Othello Sawdy, | b. Lockport, Pa., July 24, 1869. |
| | Ashtabula, Ohio. | |

39

608 Fred O. Sawdy, m. 609 Nellie Eliza Robinson, Pierpont, O.; May 7, 1890.
b. Pierpont, Ohio, June 23, 1872.

(11) C. of 608 and 609.

610 Florence Genevieve Sawdy, b. Ashtabula, Ohio, Dec. 6, 1891.

---

564 Florence A. Sawdy, m. 611 Freeman Miller, Girard, Pa., July 4, 1865.
b. Harmony, N. Y., Feb. 26, 1845.

(10) C. of 564 and 611.

612 Ina R. Miller,   b. Genoa, Olmsted Co., Minn., Feb. 26, 1869.
200 South 13th St., St. Cloud, Minn.
613 Effie Lenora Miller,   b. Winsted, Minn., Aug. 14, 1870.
614 May   "   b.   "   "   June 15, 1872.
Royalton. Minn.
615 Gertrude   "   b. Genoa, Minn., June 21, 1874.
616 Freeman   "   b.   "   "   June 9, 1876.
617 Frederick   "   b.   "   " June 9, 1876.
618 Charles Henry "   b. Alberta, Benton Co., Minn., Mar. 18, 1879.
619 Decie Lorena   "   b. Brockway, Stearns Co., Minn., July 4, 1883.
620 Conley Laverne "   b. Morril, Minn., Apr. 11, 1886.
621 James Earl   "   b. Milaca, Mille Lacs Co., Minn., June 4, '89.
622 Florence Caroline Miller, b.   "   "   "   " June 26, 1891.

---

612 Ina R. Miller, m. 623 Frank Edner Crosby, St. Cloud, Oct. 17, 1886.
b. Minneapolis, Minn., Sept. 28, 1865.

(11) C. of 612 and 623.

624 Archie Eugene Crosby, b. Brockway, Stearns Co., Minn., Sept. 12, '88.
625 A son.   b. St. Cloud, Minn., June 27, 1893.

---

614 May Miller, m. 626 Edward Reuben Smart, St. Cloud, July 19, 1888.
b. Brockway, Minn., July 19, 1865.

(11) C. of 614 and 626.

627 Florence Ruth Smart, b. Watab tp., Benton Co., Minn., June 30, 1891.
Royalton, Minn.

---

565 George H. Sawdy, m. 628 Emma Ulisa Herrick, Girard, Pa., Mar. 11, '75.
b. Girard, Pa., May 30, 1858.

(10) C. of 565 and 628.

629 A son,   b. Lockport, Pa., Sep. 1, 1876; d. Sep. 2, 1876.
630 Nellie Grace Sawdy,   b. Morrison Co., Minn., Oct. 28, 1878.
631 Laura Bell   "   b.   "   "   "   Oct. 9, 1880.
632 Ada Iown.   "   b. Girard, Pa., May 16, 1887.
    Miles Grove, Erie Co., Pa.

---

539 Samuel Sanford, m. 633 Sylvia Lovila Long, Elk Creek, Pa., Aug.
                         15, 1833.
                         b. Chesterfield, N. H., Oct. 3, 1816.
                         d. Thompson, O., Sept. 29, 1888.

(9) C. of 539 and 633.

634 Louisa Pilina Sanford,   b. Elk Creek tp., Erie Co., Pa., Mar. 9, 1835.
                                 d. Claridon, Geauga Co., O., Oct. 26, 1890.
635 Jerry Davis   "   b. Elk Creek, Pa., Oct., 22, 1836.
    Thompson, Geauga Co., Ohio.
636 Andrew Jackson Sanford, b. Madison, Lake Co., Ohio, Jan. 23, 1838.
    Carlisle, Eaton Co., Mich.
637 Marquis Lafayette Sanford, b. Madison, Ohio, Jan. 3, 1840.
                                 d. East Trumbull, Ohio, Apr. 10, 1884.
638 David Alonzo   "   b. Elk Creek, Pa., Nov., 22, 1842.
    Thompson, Ohio.
639 Asa Edgar   "   b. Madison, Ohio, Apr. 10, 1845.
    Painesville, O. (N. E. Leroy box).
640 Edward Pimpton Sanford,   b. Madison, Ohio, Aug. 24, 1847.
                                 d. Petersburg, Va., Apr. 2, 1865.
641 Daniel Samuel   "   b. Madison, Ohio, Apr. 21, 1850.
    Thompson, Ohio.
642 William Carvoso   "   b. Madison, Ohio, May 8, 1852.
                                 d. Thompson, Ohio, Nov. 6, 1884.
643 Charles Albert   "   b. Madison, Ohio, Dec. 13, 1854.
                                 d. Conneaut, Ohio, Dec. 6, 1892.
644 Mary Adelaide   "   b. Madison, Ohio, Dec. 20, 1856.
    Ashtabula, Ohio.
645 Geo. William   "   b. Madison, Ohio, Feb. 25, 1859.
                                 d.   "   "   Mar. 10, 1859.
646 Hannibal Lincoln "   b.   "   "   Nov. 22, 1860.
    Windsor Mills, Ashtabula Co., Ohio.

---

635 Jerry D. Sanford, m. 647 Lucy Miller Green, July 6, 1889.
                         b. Madison, Ohio, Jan. 9, 1832.

41

636   Andrew J. Sanford, m. 648 Sarah Jane Price, Feb. 7, 1869.
                                     b. Wayne Co., O., Mar. 27, 1849.
                                     d. Orange, Mich., Oct. 12, 1881.
                m.[2] 649 Eva Jane Bromberg, of Kalamo, Mich., June 27, 1883.
                              b. Vermontville, Mich., Feb. 14, 1862.

(10) C. of 636 and 649.

650   Raymond Bromberg Sanford, b. Orange, Ionia Co., Mich., July 30, '84.
651   Marena Ella Sanford,   b.   "   "   " May 17, 1887.
Carlisle, Eaton Co., Mich.

---

637   Marquis L. Sanford, m. 652 Mary Markt, Ionia, Mich., June 22, 1869.
                                     b. Westerburg, Germany, Nov. 23, 1849.

(10) C. of 637 and 652.

653   Alice May Sanford,   b. Thompson, Ohio, May 26, 1870.
654   Georgiana Adell "   b. Leroy, Lake Co., Ohio, April 1, 1872.
Ashtabula, Ohio.

---

654   Georgiana A. Sanford, m. 655 Jacob Orson Pinney, Lenox, Ohio,
                                  Oct. 18, 1884.
                               b. Shainlines, Pa., Sept. 23, 1858.

(11) C. of 654 and 655.

656   Linnie May Pinney,   b. Jefferson, Ashtabula Co., O., Aug. 11, 1885.
657   Ida Adell   "   b. Kingsville,   "   " Aug. 1, 1887.
                           d.   "   "   " Sept. 27, 1887.
658   Wm. Marquis "   b. Ashtabula, Ohio, Oct. 1, 1888.
                           d. Kingsville, Ohio, Dec. 1, 1889.
659   John Wesley   "   b.   "   " Nov. 29, 1889.
660   Sylvia Alice   "   b.   "   " July 6, 1892.
Kingsville, Asht. Co., Ohio.

---

638   David A. Sanford, m. 661 Minna Manley, Painesville, O., July 4, 1868.
                                  b. Concord, O., June 9, 1846; d. Apr. 28, 1876.
                m.[2] 662 Alvira Warren, Apr. 6, 1879.
                    b. Lockport, Ill., Aug. 31, 1853.

(10) C. of 638 and 661.

663   Lillian May Sanford,   b. Madison, Ohio, June 15, 1870.
664   Edward Arthur "   b.   "   " May 11, 1874.
Madison, Lake Co., Ohio.

(10) C. of 638 and 662.

665 John Henry Sanford,   b. Thompson, Ohio, Jan. 31, 1880.
666 Sylvia Mabel   "   b.   "   "   Aug. 9, 1888.
667 Edith   "   b.   "   "   Sept. 27, 1891.
                             d.   "   "   Mar. 6, 1893.

---

663 Lillian M. Sanford, m. 668 Jesse Grant Eigheny, Jefferson, O., Dec.
                             31, 1890.
                             b. Conneaut, Ohio, May 10, 1867.

(11) C. of 663 and 668.

669 Bessie Irene Eigheny,   b. Conneaut, Ohio, Sept. 26, 1891.
670 Gladys Ruth   "   b.   "   "   July 17, 1893.
Conneaut, Asht. Co., Ohio.

---

664 Edward Arthur Sanford, m. 671 Emma Snyder, Mar. 19, 1893.
                             Summit Co., Ohio, June 17, 1872.

---

639 Asa E. Sanford, m. 672 Anna Eliza Hill, Painesville, O., May 27, 1872.
                             b. Madison, Ohio, May 27, 1849.

(10) C. of 639 and 672.

673 Frank Edward Sanford, b. Leroy, Lake Co., Ohio, Oct. 19, 1873.
674 Clayton Edgar   "   b. Thompson, Ohio, Sept. 20, 1875.
675 Fay Allison   "   b.   "   "   July 18, 1878.
676 Gertrude Anna   "   b.   "   "   May 8, 1885.
                           d.   "   "   May 25, 1887.
677 Alice Elva   "   b. Leroy, Ohio, June 30, 1889.
Painesville, Ohio, (N. E. Leroy Box.)

---

641 Daniel S. Sanford, m. 678 Nettie May Gill, Thompson, O., Nov. 28, '79.
                             b. Columbus, O., Dec. 25, 1863.

(10) C. of 641 and 678.

679 Pearl Adell Sanford,   b. Thompson, Ohio, Aug. 30, 1880.
                            d.   "   "   Oct. 30, 1880.
680 Joseph Fremont   "   b.   "   "   June 17, 1882.
681 Lloyd Daniel   "   b.   "   "   Mar. 2, 1884.
682 Ethel Lovila   "   b.   "   "   July 15, 1888.
Thompson, Ohio.

---

644 Mary Adelaide Sanford, m. 683 Henry John Crook, Thompson, Ohio,
                             Jan. 1, 1878.
                             b. Brownville, N. Y., Sept. 12, 1853.

(10) **C. of 644 and 683.**

684 Louis Benjamin Crook, b. Ashtabula, Ohio, Apr. 4, 1883.
685 William Edward   "   b.   "   "   Oct. 9, 1886.
    Ashtabula, Ohio.

---

646 Hannibal L. Sanford, m. 686 Lonnettie Preston, Windsor Mills, Ohio,
                        Jan. 1, 1884.
                        b. Claridon, Ohio, Nov. 14, 1852.

(10) **C. of 646 and 686.**

687 Luthur Martin Sanford, b. Windsor, Ohio, July 6, 1888.
    Windsor Mills, Ohio.

ARMY RECORD.

Jerry D. Sanford enlisted in the spring of 1862, in the 14th Ohio Battery for a term of 3 years. Andrew J., Marquis L., and David A. Sanford, enlisted in the 15th Ohio Battery for a term of 3 years. Asa Edgar Sanford enlisted in the Fall of 1861, in 29 O. V. V. I., for 4 years. Edward Plimpton Sanford enlisted in the Fall of 1863, in Co. G., 670 O. V. V. I. for a term of 3 years, but was killed at Ft. Gregg, Petersburg, Va.

---

540 Henrietta F. Sanford, m. 688 David Webster, Erie Co., Pa., Dec. 10, '37.
                        Removed to Illinois Nov. 6, 1843.
                        b. Greenfield, N. Y., Jan. 31, 1804.
                        d. April 16, 1873.

(9) **C. of 540 and 688.**

689 Joseph Webster,   b. Erie Co., Pa., Oct. 21, 1838.
690 Hannah Millison Webster, b.   "   "   May 9, 1840.
                     d.   "   "   July 6, 1840.

---

689 Joseph Webster, m. 691 Ellen Maria Standish, of Lockport, N. Y.,
                        June 24, 1860.
                        b. Lockport, N. Y., July 23, 1842.

(10) **C. of 689 and 691.**

692 Henrietta Althea Webster, b. Sunset, Kane Co., Ill., Oct. 13, 1861.
                        d.   "   "   "   Sept. 27, 1883.
693 Harriet Lucinda   "   b.   "   "   "   Sept. 6, 1864.
                        d.   "   "   "   Sept. 28, 1885.
694 May Anneta   "   b.   "   "   "   Sept. 28, 1869.
    Elgin, Illinois.

695 Rosa Priscilla Webster,   b. Sunset, Kane Co., Ill., June 26, 1873.
                               d.   "   "   "   Feb. 4, 1876.
696 Bertie Sylvia   "   b.   "   "   "   Aug. 9, 1877.
Sunset, Kane Co., Ill.

---

692 Henrietta A. Webster, m. 697 John McBride, of Elgin, Mar. 6, 1881.
693 Harriet L. Webster, m. 698 Charles Waters, of Ind., Nov. 7, 1883.
694 May A. Webster, m. 699 Charles Beatie, Oct. 6, 1888.
                    b. Hampshire, Kane Co., Ill., Sept. 25, 1868.

(11) C. of 694 and 699.

700 Laura Mabel Beatie,   b. Sunset, Ill., Mar. 26, 1892.
701 ———   "   b.   "   "   May 9, 1893.

---

541 Caroline Sanford, m. 702 Gustavus Keith, about 1838 ; d. about 1865.

(9) C. of 541 and 702.

703 Sarah Ella Keith,   b. 1850.
Elyria, Ohio.
703 Sarah Ella Keith, m. 704 William Foley.

(10) C. of 703 and 704.

705
706
707
708
709

---

542 Nehemiah Sanford, m. 710 Anice Tryphosa Rich, Mar. 14, 1850.
                    b. Rutland, Vt., Sept. 21, 1830.
                    d. Elgin, Ill., March 29, 1881.
                m.[2] 711 Cornelia Benedict, Sept. 22, 1882.
                    b. Mich., Dec. 24, 1830.
                    d. Council Bluffs, Iowa, Feb. 16, 1890.

---

543 David Sanford, m. 712 Lucinda Stillwell, July 4, 1849.
                  b. Aug. 12, 1823 ; d. Sept. 30, 1887.

(9) C. of 543 and 712.

713 Wm. Bradford Sanford, b. Elk Creek tp., Pa., Sept. 20, 1850.
Lundy's Lane, Pa.
714 Alvin Thayer   "   b.   "   "   Oct. 1, 1851.
Platea, Erie Co., Pa.
715 Rachel Maria Sanford, b. Lockport, Erie Co., Pa. Dec. 31, 1854.
Lundy's Lane, Pa.

716	Eva Lucinda Sanford,	b. Girard, Pa., March 31, 1857.
		d. Nov. 18, 1875.
717	Andrew Granville "	b. Girard, Pa., Oct. 20, 1858.
	Lundy's Lane, Pa.	
718	John David "	b. Lockport, Pa.; July 28, 1860.
	Conneaut, Ohio.	
719	Levi Henry "	b. Lockport, Pa., June 18, 1865.
	Lundy's Lane, Pa.	

714 Alvin T. Sanford, m. 720 Amanda Peckham, July 4, 1873.

  b. N. Y. State, June 3, 1855 ; divorced 1880.

  m.² 721 Mrs. Adaline Davenport, March 12, 1881.

  b. Jan. 28, 1851.

(10) C. of 714 and 720.

722	Charles Sanford,	b. Lockport, Pa., March 12, 1874.
	Girard, Pa.	
723	Edward Sanford,	b. " " June 5, 1876.
	Platea, Pa.	

722 Charles Sanford, m. 724 Nellie Mathews, Oct. 15, 1892.

  b. Girard, Pa., Feb. 10, 1873.

715 Rachel M. Sanford, m. 725 William T. Gregory, June 2, 1877.

  b. Elk Creek, Pa., Nov. 2, 1848.

(10) C. of 715 and 725.

726	William David Gregory,	b. Lundy's Lane, Pa., May 20, 1878.
727	Lee "	b. " " Dec. 20, 1887.
	Lundy's Lane, Pa.	

716 Eva Lucinda Sanford, m. 725 William T. Gregory, Sept. 10, 1873.

717 Andrew G. Sanford, m. 728 Harriet Emma Richardson, Feb. 8, 1880.

  b. Westford, N. Y., Nov. 20, 1857.

(10) C. of 717 and 728.

729	Glenn David Sanford,	b. Elk Creek, Pa., Sept. 10, 1890.
	Lundy's Lane, Pa.	

718 John D. Sanford, m. 730 Sarah Deyoe, Dec. 25, 1883.

  b. Conneaut, Ohio, Sept. 15, 1862.

(10) C. of 718 and 730.

731 Eva May Sanford,   b. Conneaut, Ohio, May 1, 1888.
732 Earl Lemon "   b.   "   "   Aug. 8, 1890.
    Conneaut, Ohio.

---

719 Levi H. Sanford, m. 733 Maud Halstead, March 30, 1890.
                        b. Lockport, Pa., Feb. 15, 1866.

(10) C. of 719 and 733.

734 Roy Sanford,   b. Elk Creek, Pa., Sept, 27, 1891.
735 Clyde "   b.   "   "   March 15, 1893.
    Lundy's Lane, Pa.

---

544 Sophia Sanford, m. 736 Calvin Carr, Aug. 27, 1840.
                   b. Vt., June 21, 1817.
              m.² 737 John Bogart, Conneautville, Pa., Aug. 3, 1871.

(9) C. of 544 and 736.

738	Lester Pernet Carr, Erie, Pa.		b. Lockport, Erie Co., Pa., May 26, 1841.					
739	Willard Emery	"	b.	"	"	"	June 15, 1844.
			d.	"	"	"	Nov. 10, 1847.
740	Polly Priscilla	"	b.	"	"	"	Jan. 15, 1845.
741	Abigail Diantha	"	b.	"	"	"	Sept. 6, 1848.
			d.	"	"	"	June 16, 1877.
742	John Adrial	"	b.	"	"	"	Oct. 20, 1850.
			d.	"	"	"	Dec. 28, 1875.
743	Orvil Orlando	"	b.	"	"	"	Oct. 5, 1853.
744	Mary Louisa	"	b.	"	"	"	June 10, 1855.
			d.	"	"	"	Jan. 26, 1857.
745	Emma Jane Conneaut, Ohio.	"	b.	"	"	"	July 8, 1857.
746	Cassius Casper	"	b.	"	"	"	Oct. 23, 1859.
747	Freddie Wilmot	"	b.	"	"	"	July 8, 1861.
			d.	"	"	"	Nov. 24, 1863.
748	Elmer Elsworth	"	b.	"	"	"	Sept. 11, 1863.
			d.	"	"	"	Sept. 5, 1864.
749	Frank Delbert	"	b.	"	"	"	May 28, 1865.

788 Lester P. Carr, m. 750 Mary M. Simmons, 1865.

(10) C. of 738 and 750.

751	Mark Augustus Carr,	b.	Girard, Pa., 1867.
752	Claude "	b.	" " 1869.
753	Hattie "	b.	" " 1871.
754	Vernie Dillion "	b.	" " 1876.
		d.	Erie, Pa., April 26, 1887.
755	Nellie "	b.	Girard, Pa., 1878.
756	Archie "	b.	Erie, Pa., 1886.
757	Mamie "	b.	" 1887.

740 Polly P. Carr, m. 758 Thomas Lamb, April 20, 1863 ; d. 1877.
m.² 759 Brice Shuart.

(10) C. of 740 and 758.

760	Ella Lamb,	b.	May 7, 1864.
761	Leda "	b.	July 22, 1866.
762	Thomas"	b.	July 3, 1876.
		d.	Dec. 15, 1883.

(10) C. of 740 and 759.

763	Bessie Shuart,	b.	July 10, 1884.
764	Augusta Olean Shuart,	b.	Aug. 14, 1888.
		d.	June 10, 1890.

743 Orvil O. Carr, m. 765 Martha Benden.
b. Jan. 21, 1855.

(10) C. of 743 and 765.

766	James Calvin Carr,	b.	May 18, 1876.
767	Freddie Wilmot "	b.	Feb. 17, 1878 ; d. July 10, 1887.
768	Alma Blanche "	b.	Jan. 1, 1880.
769	George Orland "	b.	Aug. 17, 1881.
770	William "	b.	July 11, 1889.

745 Emma J. Carr, m. 771 Charles Lilley, Springfield, Pa., Aug. 10, 1878.

(10) C. of 745 and 771.

772	Carl Casper Lilley,	b.	Conneaut, Ohio, June 4, 1879.
773	Maud May "	b.	" " Sept. 10, 1881.
774	Roy Lee "	b.	" " May 2, 1893.
		d.	" " Aug. 20, 1893.

545 Elizabeth Sanford, m. 775 Rufus H. Hatch, Elk Creek, Pa., Dec. 18,'49.
b. Salem, Wash. Co., N. Y., May 16, 1822.

(9) C. of 545 and 775.

776	Clara I. Hatch,	b.	Conneaut, Ohio,	Jan. 5, 1852.
777	Lydia "	b.	"	"	Nov. 1, 1855.
		d.	"	"	Aug. 30, 1861.
778	Leamon C. Hatch,	b.	"	"	Nov. 24, 1860.
		d.	"	"	Jan. 28, 1888.

776 Clara I. Hatch, m. 779 Miner C. Moon, Conneaut, O., Dec. 25, 1873.
b. Ticonderoga, N. Y., March 29, 1843.

(10) C. of 776 and 779.

780	Lizzie E. Moon,	b.	Cleveland, Ohio,	Dec. 5, 1879.
781	Henry H. "	b.	"	"	Oct. 22, 1882.
		d.	"	"	Nov. 21, 1889.

778 Leamon C. Hatch, m. 782 Bertie Morehead, Cleveland, O., Jan. 21,'85.
b. Greenwich, Ohio, Feb. 4, 1866.

(10) C. of 778 and 782.

783	Cornelia Hatch,	b. Cleveland, Ohio, April 20, 1886.
784	Home Lee "	b. Indianapolis, Ind., Oct. 17, 1887.

546 Alvin Thayer Sanford, m. 785 Sarah Jane Spicer, Sept. 9, 1849.
b. Conneaut, O., July 19, 1829; d. July 1, '66.
m.[2] 786 Mert Spicer, Aug. 1866.
b. April 7, 1844.

(9) C. of 546 and 785.

787	Alida Isadore Sanford,	b.	Elk Creek, Pa.,	Oct. 29, 1852.
788	George Ellis "	b.	"	"	May 11, 1858.
789	James W. "	b.	"	"	Nov. 27, 1860.
		d.	"	"	April 24, 1861.
790	Warren Philip "	b.	"	"	Jan. 22, 1862.

(9) C. of 546 and 786.

791	William J. Sanford,	b.	Elk Creek, Pa., July 16, 1867.
792	Lindia May "	b.	Conneaut, Ohio, Aug. 22, 1869.
793	Mertie Estella " .	b.	"	"	June 26, 1873.
	Conneaut, Ohio.				

787 Alida I. Sanford, m. 794 Burton Tinker, July 4, 1871.
b. May 27, 1852.

49

(10) **C. of 787 and 794.**

795 Minnie May Tinker, b. Conneaut, Ohio, Sept. 18, 1872.
796 Addie Jane " " b. Kingsville, Ohio, May 23, 1876.

795 Minnie M. Tinker, m. 797 Henry A. Buss, Conneaut, O., Nov. 17, 1891.
    b. Sand Beach, Mich., May 27, 1868.

788 George E. Sanford, m. 798 Lena McLaughlin, March 7, 1878.
    b. Beaver, Pa., March 15, 1862.

(10) **C. of 788 and 798.**

799 Arthur Sanford, b. Conneaut, Ohio, Nov. 21, 1879.
800 Irene " b. " " Aug. 16, 1889.

790 Warren P. Sanford, m. 801 Carrie Laura Prince, July 2, 1881.
    b. Pierpont, Ohio. May 12, 1863.

(10) **C. of 790 and 801.**

802 Wavie Lavina Sanford, b. Pierpont, Asht. Co., O., Feb. 15, 1882.
803 Raymond Hardy " b. Conneaut, Ohio, June 20, 1884.
804 Jessie Prince " b. " " April 5, 1889.
805 Harland " b. " " April 21, 1892.

791 William J. Sanford, m. 806 Katie Morton, Oct. 26, 1889.
    b. May 26, 1872.

(10) **C. of 791 and 806.**

807 Lorna Kate Sanford, b. Conneaut, Ohio, Dec. 27, 1890.
808 Enid Osene " b. " " Sept. 18, 1892.

792 Lindia M. Sanford, m. 809 Wm. Judson Bancroft, Sept. 27, 1890.
    b. Jan. 5, 1871.

(10) **C. of 792 and 809.**

810 Irma May Bancroft, b. Conneaut, Ohio, May 31, 1892.

793 Mertie E. Sanford, m. 811 John Heman Dewey, May 11, 1892.
    b. Jefferson, Ohio, July 5, 1871.

548 Isaac Sanford, m. 812 Olive Spicer, June 1, 1854.
    b. Albion, Pa., 1832 ; d. July 28, 1865.
    m.[2] 813 Catharine Doyle, Springfield, Pa., Dec. 25, 1865.
    b. Nov. 27, 1837.

(9) C. of 548 and 812.

814	Lemuel J. Sanford,	b. Girard, Pa., May 7, 1855.
		d. " " Oct. 18, 1863.
815	Patience Alzora "	b. " " Oct. 6 1856.
	Shelby, Oceana Co., Mich.	
816	William Henry Sanford, b.	" " July 28, 1858.
	Shelby, Mich.	
817	Fred Breckenridge "	b. " " July 24, 1860.
	Shelby, Mich.	
818	Franklin Pierce "	b. " " July 24, 1860.
	Newaygo, Mich.	
819	Lydia Jane "	b. " " Oct. 4, 1862.
	Kingsville, Ohio.	
820	Delia "	b. " " July 14, 1865.
	Conneaut, Ohio.	
821	Celia "	b. " " July 14, 1865.
		d. " " Aug. 28, 1865.

(9) C. of 548 and 813.

822	Elroy Sanford,	b. Conneaut, Ohio, Nov. 26, 1867.
		d. E. Conneaut, Dec. 17, 1868.
823	Hiram Sawdy Sanford,	b. Conneaut, June 3, 1869.
824	Wallace Leroy "	b. " Aug. 15, 1871.
825	Epho Estella "	Springfield, Pa., Sept. 25, 1875.

815 Patience A. Sanford, m. 826 Francis Jerome Clark, W. Springfield, Pa., June 25, 1873.
b. Monroe, Asht. Co., Ohio, March 5, 1849.

(10) C. of 815 and 826.

827	Bert LeRoy Clark,	b. Kelloggsville, Ohio, May 20, 1875.
828	Olive Adell "	b. Sunfield, Mich., July 26, 1877.
829	Elroy Jay "	b. " " March 26, 1879.
830	Warren Dennis Clark,	b. Golden, Mich., Sept. 15, 1882.

816 William H. Sanford, m. 831 Ollia Ann Frasure, June 30, 1880.
b. Richmond, Ohio, Feb. 24, 1861.

(10) C. of 816 and 831.

832	Jesse Carl Sanford,	b. Hart, Oceana Co., Mich., May 13, 1881.
		d. " " " Oct. 28, 1881.
833	Harry Adelbert "	b. " " " Sept. 2, 1882.
		d. " " " Feb. 18, 1885.
834	Ardie Leland "	b. Shelby, " " July 22, 1889.

51

817 .Fred B. Sanford, m. 835 Ida Elizabeth Lintz, Hart, Mich., July 3, '80.
  b. Amherst, N. Y., March 25, 1864.

(10) C. of 817 and 835.

836 Celia Augusta Sanford, b. Golden, Mich., July 23, 1882.
837 James Blaine " b. Hart, Mich., Feb. 12, 1884. .
838 Pearl Clayton " b. " " March 20, 1886.
839 Elsie Triola " b. Shelby, " Sept. 27, 1887.
840 Mina Luella " b. " " May 12, 1889.

818 Franklin.P. Sanford, m. 841 Rosetta Amanda Briggs, March 9, 1889.
  b. Newaygo, Mich., March 14, 1871.

(10) C. of 818 and 841.

842 George Isaac Sanford, b. Newaygo, Mich., March 30, 1890.
843 Edith Gertrude, " b. " " May 14, 1891.

819 Lydia J. Sanford, m. 844 Daniel Russell Squires, Sept. 10, 1882.
  b. Asht. Co., Ohio, March 6, 1856.

(10) C. of 819 and 844.

845 Burt Russell Squires, b. Kingsville, Ohio, July 23, 1884,
846 Maud May " b. " " Feb. 18, 1887.
847 Grace A. " b. " " Nov. 22, 1888.
848 Lucy " b. " " Aug. 5, 1892.

820 Delia Sanford, m. 849 Joseph Lillie Risley, Conneaut, O., Dec. 25, '84.
  b. Denmark, Ohio, Aug. 28, 1862.

(10) C. of 820 and 849.

850 Herman Henry Risley, b. Conneaut, Ohio, Feb. 6, 1893.

823 Hiram S. Sanford. m. 851 Mina Blohm. Hart, Mich., Sept. 6, 1889.
  b. LaPorte, Ind., March 22, 1872.

(10) C. of 823 and 851.

852 Leo Newton Sanford, b. Shelby, Mich., March 31, 1891.

824 Wallace L. Sanford, m. 853 Emma Gregory, Shelby, Mich., Aug. 15,'90.

59　Peleg Sanford, m. 854 Eliza Anderson, Eaton, N. Y., 1817. (?)
　　　　　　　　　　　　b. Sept. 16, 1800.
　　　　　　　　　　　　d. Clark Co., Ill., June 23. 1829.
　　　　　　m.² 855 Malinda Greenlief, Madison, N. Y., March 23, 1832.
　　　　　　　　　　　　b. Oct. 16, 1804.
　　　　　　　　　　　　d. Lincoln, Wash., Aug. 30, 1892.

(8) C. of 59 and 854.

856　Peleg Anderson Sanford, b. Madison, N. Y., Jan., 20, 1818.
　　　　　　　　　　　　d. Reynolds' Station, Ind., May 11, 1858.
857　William Henry　　　"　b. Madison, N. Y., April 18, 1819.
　　Hoopeston, Ill.
858　James Madison　　　"　b.　　"　　　"　Nov. 20, 1820.
　　1723 S. 2d St., Terre Haute, Ind.
859　Thomas Wesley Sanford, b.　　"　　　"　Aug. 30, 1822.
　　　　　　　　　　　　d. Clark Co., Ill., March 16, 1847.
860　Amanda Malvina　　"　b.　　"　　　"　July 20, 1824.
　　　　　　　　　　　　d.　　"　　　"　July,21, 1824.
861　Lucetta Ann　　　　"　b.　　"　　　"　Oct. 16, 1825.
　　　　　　　　　　　　d.　　"　　　"　Sept. 10, 1826.
862　America Ogelsby　　"　b.　　"　　　"　Dec. 20, 1827.
　　West Lebanon, Ind.

(8) C. of 59 and 855.

863　Tilley Greenlief Sanford, b. Clark Co., Ill., Jan. 3, 1834.
　　Lincoln, Douglas Co., Wash.
864　Mary Eliza Sanford,　　b.　　"　　　"　Jan. 7, 1836.
　　　　　　　　　　　　d.　　"　　　"　Aug. 16, 1836.
865　John Herman　"　　b.　　"　,　"　Dec. 16, 1837.
　　Moscow, Idaho.
866　Israel Liberty Sanford,　b. Vigo Co., Ind., Sept. 20, 1840.
　　Lincoln, Douglas Co., Wash.
867　Harriet Sanford,　　　b.　　"　　　"　Sept. 20, 1840.
　　　　　　　　　　　　d.　　"　　　"　Sept. 20, 1840.
868　Albert Marion Sanford,　b.　　"　　　"　July 21, 1843.
　　　　　　　　　　　　d.　　"　　　"　Nov. 21, 1844.
869　Alonzo Lapham　　"　b. Clark Co., Ill., Nov. 2, 1845.
　　Covello, Columbia Co., Wash.
870　Christopher Abraham Sanford, b. "　　"　May 2, 1849.
　　Beresford, Union Co., S. Dakota.

856　Peleg A. Sanford, m. 871 Emeline Marvin, Dec. 26, 1839.
　　　　　　　　　　　　b. Onondaga Co., N. Y., March 14, 1824.
　　　　　　　　　　　　　P. O., Stafford, Kans.

53

(9) C. of 856 and 871.

872	Owen Clay Sanford, Stafford, Kan.	b. Vigo Co., Ind., Aug. 17, 1842.
873	Albert Eli Sanford,	b. Darwin, Clark Co., Ill., April 21, 1845. d. Covington, Ind., August 19, 1846.
874	Ann Eliza "	b. Covington, " July 8, 1847. d. Darwin, Ill., Nov. 20, 1863.
875	Wm. Winfield Sanford, Wichita, Kans.	b. Covington, Ind., Aug. 12, 1852.
876	Amanda Emeline " Stafford, Kans.	b. Crawfordsville, Ind., Aug. 16, 1856.
877	James Anderson "	b. " " Aug. 16, 1856. d. Clark Co., Ill., Sept. 16, 1862.

---

872 Owen C. Sanford, m. 878 Elizabeth Ann Parvis, Dec. 24, 1863.
b. Tippecanoe Co., Ind., Sept. 13, 1846.
d. Oct. 29, 1882.
m.² 879 Leota Levina Roberts, Sept. 19, 1847.
b. Kasson, Dodge Co., Minn., Dec. 16, 1870.

(10) C. of 872 and 878.

879	Charles Albert Sanford,	b. Darwin, Ill., Nov. 11, 1864.
880	Launa Bell "	b. " " Nov. 7, 1866. d. " " Jan. 31, 1888.
881	Harry Homer "	b. " " Feb. 27, 1869. d. " " Oct. 18, 1875.
882	William Anderson "	b. " " Nov. 3, 1874. d. " " Feb. 21, 1877.
883	Zoula Gertrude "	b. " " April 7, 1879.

(10) C. of 872 and 879.

884	Ina Ethel Sanford,	b. Wichita, Kans., Aug. 11, 1889.
885	Owen Clyde "	b. Stafford, Kans., April 20, 1892.

---

879 Charles Albert Sanford, m. 886 Mary Magnola Vice, Aug. 26, 1889.
Bath Co., Ky,, Dec. 27, 1867.

(11) C. of 879 and 886.

887 Owen Anderson Sanford, b. Stafford, Kans., May 27, 1891.

---

880 Launa Bell Sanford, m. 888 William Lyman Munger, Aug. 25, 1886.
b. July 7, 1860.

(11) C. of 880 and 888.

889   Launa Ethel Munger,   b. Stafford, Kans., Jan. 21, 1888.
                                   d.   "   "   Dec. 8, 1890.

---

874   Ann Eliza Sanford, m. 899 Daniel J. Davidson, Dec. 25, 1862.

---

875   William Winfield Sanford, m. 891 Linnie Gwendowin Martin, Wichita,
                    Kans., Oct. 10, 1881.
                    b. Plymouth, Richland Co., O., Feb. 17, '63.

(10) C. of 875 and 891.

892   Beatrice Raymond Sanford, b. Wichita, Kans., Jan. 31, 1883.
893   Audrey St. Clair   "   b.   "   "   Sept. 28, 1884.

---

876   Amanda E. Sanford, m. 894 Alfred Irvin Higgins, May 9, 1875.

(10) C. of 876 and 894.

895   Edna Amanda Higgins,   b. Urbana, Champaign Co., Ill., June 26,'78.

---

857   William Henry Sanford, m. 896 Rachel Ogden. Clark Co., Ill., Dec.
                    19, 1854.
                    b. Clark Co., Ill., May 3, 1832.
                    d. Union Co., Iowa, July 30, 1866.
             m.² 897 Mary Brewer Lynch, March 23, 1869.
                    b. Brown Co., O., Nov. 16, 1819.
                    d. July 29, 1878.

(9) C. of 857 and 896.

898   Florence Sanford,   b. Fountain Co., Ind., March 18, 1856.
                                d. Hoopeston, Ill., Nov. 1, 1859.
899   Homer   "   b. Fountain Co., Ind., Feb. 16, 1858.
        Hoopeston, Ind.
900   Ethlen Etta Sanford,   b. State Line City, Ind., March 29, 1861.
        Catlin, Ill.
901   Mary Jane   "   b. Warren Co., Ind., Jan. 31, 1864.
                                 d. Georgetown, Ill., April 1, 1892.
902   Emma Ann   "   ,   b. Union Co., Iowa, Sept. 9, 1865.
                               d.   "   "   Aug. 19, 1866.

---

899   Homer Sanford, m. 903 Sarah Ann Bloomfield, Hoopeston, Aug. 24,'84.
                    b. Vermilion Co., Ill., March 29, 1861.

---

900 Ethlen Etta Sanford, m. 905 Albert Clipson, Jan. 24, 1889.
        b. Vermilion Co., Ill., Nov. 25, 1854.

(10) C. of 900 and 905.

906 Homer Albert Clipson,   b. Vermilion Co., Ill., Jan. 19, 1890.
Catlin, Ill.

---

901 Mary Jane Sanford, m. 907 Henry D. Smith, Hoopeston, Mar. 19, '84.
        b. McLean Co., Ill., Feb. 17, 1863.
             P. O., Georgetown, Ill.

(11) C. of 901 and 907.

908 Myrtle May Smith,   b. Vermilion Co., Ill., Jan. 1, 1855.
Georgetown, Ill.
909 Oscar Everett Smith,   b.   "   "   April 3, 1888.
            d.   "   "   April 4, 1888.
910 Walter A.   "   b.   "   "   April 4, 1890.
910² Minnie Jane   "   b.   "   "   March 25, 1892.

---

858 James M. Sanford, m. 911 Elizabeth Precious Lloyd, May 9, 1844.
        b. Nov. 16, 1823.

(9) C. of 858 and 911.

912 William Peleg Sanford,   b. Sullivan Co., Ind., Feb. 3, 1845.
Terre Haute, Ind.
913 Warren Anderson   "   b. Clark Co., Ill., Feb. 25, 1847.
Youngstown, Ind.
914 Margaret Jane   "   b. Sullivan Co., Ind., Nov. 17, 1848.
Terre Haute, Ind.
915 America Emeline   "   b.   "   "   Nov. 17, 1848.
           d. Vigo Co., Ind., March 17, 1865.
916 James Byron   "   b. Shelburn, Sull. Co., Ind., Oct. 17, 1850.
           d.   "   "   "   April 18, 1851.
917 Winfield Grable   "   b.   "   "   "   July 28, 1852.
New Goshen, Ind.
918 Webster Sanford,   b. Youngstown, Vigo Co., Ind., May 15, 1855.
           d.   "   "   " May 17, 1855.
919 Walter   "   b.   "   "   " May 15, 1855.
           d.   "   "   " June 3, 1855.
920 Matilda   "   b.   "   "   " May 15, 1855.
           d.   "   "   " May 31, 1855.
921 Wilton Thomas Sanford, b.   "   "   " Sept. 6, 1856.
Terre Haute, Ind.
922 Joseph Miller Sanford,   b.   "   "   " Jan. 31, 1859.
Youngstown, Ind.

923 James Coleman Sanford, b. Youngstown, Vigo Co., Ind., July 22, 1861.
            d.   "   "   " Mar. 23, 1865.
924 Mary Elizabeth   "   b.   "   "   " July 22, 1861.
    Pimento, Ind.

---

912 William P. Sanford, m. 925 Eliza Jane McCoskey, April 5, 1870.
            b. August 9, 1851.

(10) C. of 912 and 925.

926 Carrie Almina Sanford, b. Vigo Co., Ind., Feb. 18, 1871.
    Pimento, Ind.
927 Elmer Anderson   "   b.   "   " Oct. 25, 1873.
    Terre Haute, Ind.
928 Elizabeth Anna   "   b.   "   " Dec. 28, 1876.
                 d.   "   " Jan. 18, 1879.
929 Winfield Porter   "   b.   "   " Jan. 26, 1881.
    Terre Haute, Ind.
930 Minnie Valora   "   b.   "   " July 18, 1884.
    Terre Haute, Ind.

---

926 Carrie A. Sanford, m. 931 John Wesley Boyle, May 11, 1890.
            b. near Pimento, Ind., Oct. 14, 1867.

---

913 Warren A. Sanford, m. 932 Sarah J. Whitaker, who died April, 1873.
         m.[2] 933 Flora Cecil Hassinger, Vigo Co., Ind., Nov. 23, '82.
         b. Warren Co., Ohio, May 22, 1860.
         d. Youngstown, Ind., Jan. 29, 1892.

(10) C. of 913 and 933.

934 Floyd Roscoe Sanford,   b. Riley, Vigo Co., Ind., Aug. 31, 1883.
935 Leo Wayne   "   b. Maxville,   "   " Sept. 6, 1886.
936 Flora Cecil   "   b.   "   "   " Dec. 28, 1891.
                 d.   "   "   " April, 1892.

---

914 Margaret J. Sanford, m. 937 Andrew Ferdinand Winn, Nov. 17, 1885.
            b. Muskingum Co., Ohio, Dec. 6, 1849.

---

917 Winfield G. Sanford, m. 938 Charrie Olive Hay, Vermilion, Ill., Mar.
         23, 1881.
         b. Clinton, Vermilion Co., Ind., May 20, '60.

(10) C. of 917 and 938.

939 Rose Gertrude Sanford,   b. New Goshen, Vigo Co., Ind., Oct. 16, '85.
940 Margaret Blanche   "   b. Terre Haute, Ind., Aug. 22, 1887.
941 John McKinley   "   b. New Goshen,   "   Nov. 10, 1893.

921 Wilton T. Sanford, m. 942 Nancy Etta Littlejohn, Riley, Vigo Co., Ind.,
Sept. 21, 1885.

(10) C. of 921 and 942.

943 Homer Clement Sanford, b. Youngstown, Vigo Co., Ind., Aug. 19, '86.
                                d.   "   "   " Nov. 8, '92.
944 Loren Alvis   "   b. Terre Haute, Ind., Feb. 10, 1889.
945 Valeria May   "   b.   "   " May, 1892.

---

922 Joseph M. Sanford, m. 946 Martha B. Young, Youngstown, Ind.,
Feb. 26, 1880.
b. Vigo Co., Ind., Sept. 18, 1864.

(10) C. of 922 and 946.

947 Nellie Alma Sanford,   b. Youngstown, Ind., May 4, 1881.
948 Howard William Sanford, b.   "   " Oct. 22, 1883.
949 Joe Dana   "   b.   "   " Jan. 15, 1886.
                                d.   "   " Nov. 22, 1892.
950 Herman Harrison   "   b.   "   " May 29, 1888.
951 Herbert Heman   "   b.   "   " May 13, 1890.

---

924 Mary E. Sanford, m. 952 James Allen Heady, Oct. 30, 1887.
b. Vigo Co., Ind., Sept. 3, 1858.

(10) C. of 924 and 952.

953 William Oscar Heady,   b. Pimento, Ind., April 8, 1891.

---

862 America O. Sanford, m. 954 Wm. McClure Logan, Fountain Co., Ind.,
Sept. 2, 1847.
b. Ohio, April 10, 1821.
d. Allen Co., Kans., Oct. 23, 1862.

(9) C. of 862 and 954.

955 Horace Alexander Logan, b. Fountain Co., Ind., July 28, 1848.
956 Eliza Alice   " b.   "   " July 21, 1850.
West Lebanon, Ind.
957 Emma Lauretta   " b.   "   " Oct. 18, 1852.
Danville, Ill.
958 Mary Evaline   " b.   "   " Feb. 22, 1855.
959 Florence Anna   " b. Mercer Co., Ill., Nov. 8, 1857.
Boswell, Benton Co., Ind.
960 Rosetta Jane Sanford,   b. Allen Co., Kans., March 18, 1862.
d. Fountain Co., Ind., April 16, 1863.

---

859 Florence A. Logan, m. 961 Runic Welton Alexander, Oct. 11, 1882.
b. Warren Co., Ind., March 9, 1860.

(10) C. of 859 and 961.

962 Joe Allen Alexander,   b. State Line City, Ind., April 15, 1884.
963 Earl Logan   "   b. Warren Co., Ind., Jan. 18, 1891.
Boswell, Benton Co., Ind.
964 Ray Hanks Alexander, b   "   "   Aug. 4, 1892.

---

863 Tilley G. Sanford, m. 965 Dora Millage, Lincoln, Dak., Aug. 15, 1877.
b. N. Y., August 7, 1859.

(9) C. of 863 and 965.

966 Louisa Malinda Sanford, b. Lincoln Co., Dak., Jan. 10, 1879.
967 Emma   "   b.   "   "   Jan. 23, 1881.
968 Julia   "   b. Columbia Co., Wash., June 1, 1883.
969 Ella   "   b. Douglas Co., Wash., Jan. 21, 1885.
970 Mary   "   b.   "   "   July 14, 1887.
971 Byron   "   b.   "   "   March 28, 1889.
972 Lucinda   "   b.   "   "   May 4, 1892.

---

865 John H. Sanford, m. 973 Mary Jane Nelson, March 6, 1866.
b. Mich., Nov. 9, 1848.

(9) C. of 865 and 973.

974 Violet S. Sanford,   b. Boone Co., Iowa, Dec. 4, 1867.
975 Geo. Wm. Henry Sanford, b.   "   "   April 23, 1870.
    d.   "   "   Jan. 14, 1872.
976 Charles Marion   "   b.   "   "   Jan. 2, 1873.
977 James Albertus   "   b. Lincoln Co., S. Dak., Feb. 29, 1876.
    d.   "   "   March 3, 1880.
978 John LeRoy   "   b.   "   "   Sept. 24, 1878.
979 Mary Alice   "   b.   "   "   Feb. 26, 1881.
980 Wm. Sherman   "   b.   "   "   April 11, 1883.
981 Jesse Harold   "   b.   "   "   Oct. 12, 1888.

---

976 Charles M. Sanford, m. 982 Ella Olson, Feb. 22, 1893.
b. S. Dak., March 27, 1874.

---

866 Israel L. Sanford, m. 983 Nettie Millage, Lincoln Co., S. Dak., Jan.
3, 1882.
b. N. Y., April 1, 1863.

(9) C. of 866 and 983.

984	Rosa Sanford,	b. Columbia Co., Wash., June 10, 1883.
985	Lilly Bell "	b. " " Aug. 10, 1885.
986	James "	b. " " June 27, 1887.
987	Frank "	b. " " Sept. 8, 1889.
988	George W. "	b. " " Nov. 17, 1891.

869   Alonzo L. Sanford, m. 989 Alice Malinda McBride, March 15, 1881.
                       b. Monroe Co., Iowa, June 30, 1859.

(9) C. of 869 and 989.

990	Wilson Greenlief Sanford, b. Columbia Co., Wash., April 18, 1882.
991	Caroline Malinda " b. " " Dec. 18, 1883.
	d. " " Nov. 1. 1891.
992	Bertrand " b. " " April 19, 1886.
993	Christopher Brady " b. " " Aug. 22, 1888.
994	Pearl Bertha " b. " " April 16, 1891.
995	Estella Jane " b. " " Sept. 21, 1892.

870   Christopher A. Sanford, m. 996 Agnes Mary Weitzell, Meckling, S.
                 Dak., Sept. 20, 1873.
                 b. Cedarville, Stephenson Co., Ill., Mar. 2, 1857.

(9) C. of 870 and 996.

997	Fredress Irene Sanford,	b. Meckling, S. Dak., Jan. 10, 1875.
998	Sebastian W. A. "	b. Brooklyn, " July 4, 1877.
		d. " " April 15, 1891.
999	Maud A. "	b. Meckling, " June 10, 1879.
1000	Pearl Grace "	b. Brooklyn, " Aug. 12, 1881.
1001	Alfred L. "	b. " " Oct. 20, 1883.
1002	Richard S. "	b. " " Nov. 12, 1885.
1003	Ethel May "	b. " " Feb. 29, 1887.

60   Nancy Sanford, m. 1004 Philip Russell, Madison, N. Y., Nov. 1808.
                 b. Cornwall, Ct., Sept. 12, 1787.
                 d. Windham, Ohio, July 1, 1879.

(8) C. of 60 and 1004.

1005	Nancy Russell,	b. Hamilton, N. Y., Aug. 2, 1809.
	Windham, Ohio.	
1006	Philip Russell, Jr.,	b. " " Oct. 25, 1811.
		d. Windham, Ohio, Feb. 19, 1886.

1007	Peleg Russell,		b. Hamilton, N. Y., Oct. 20, 1813.
			d. " " April 13, 1814.
1008	Daniel "		b. " " Feb. 1, 1815.
			d. Windham, Ohio, Feb. 6, 1823.
1009	Abigail S. Russell,		b. Nelson, " July 25, 1818.
			d. Cleveland, " Nov. 25, 1846.
1010	Electa A. "		b. Nelson, " Feb. 12, 1821.
1011	William "		b. Windham, " . Aug. 21, 1823.
			d. " " Oct. 25, 1825.
1012	Wm. Sanford "		b. . " " Feb. 15, 1826.
	Newton Falls, Trumbull Co., O.		
1013	Daniel Abram Russell,		b. " " Mar. 5, 1828.
	Vineland, N. J.		
1014	Mary Lucretia "		b. " " Aug. 12, 1830.
			d. " " Sept. 1, 1871.
1015	Madison J. "		b. " " April 1, 1833.
	California.		
1016	Delia E. "		b. " " Oct. 2, 1835.
	Windham, Ohio.		
1017	Webster B. "		b. " " Jan. 27, 1838.
	Boscobel, Wis.		

1005 Nancy Russell, m. 1018 Edmond Yale, Windham, O., Feb. 7, 1833.
b. Canfield, Ohio, Sept. 4, 1806.
d. Windham, Ohio, Aug. 3, 1878.

(9) C. of 1005 and 1018.

1019	Edwin Yale,		b. Windham, Ohio, Dec. 3, 1833.
			d. " " Dec. 29, 1846.
1020	Celia "		b. " " June 11, 1836.
			d. " " Dec. 13, 1868.
1021	Sanford Strong Yale,		b. " " Sept. 10, 1841.
			d. Camp Chase," Dec. 25, 1861.
1022	Samuel S. "		b. Windham, Ohio, Sept. 15, 1844.
	Windham, O.		
1023	A son,		b. " " Feb. 19, 1849.
			d. " " May 15, 1849.

1020 Celia Yale, m. 1024 Roswell Cutts, Windham, Ohio, Dec. 12, 1864.
b. Paris, O., Oct. 3, 1840 ; P. O., Hiram, O.

1022 Samuel S. Yale, m. 1025 Sevilla S. Shively, Lordstown, O., Sept. 5, '67.
b. Bristol, Ohio, March 30, 1848.

61

(10) C. of 1022 and 1025.

1026	Edmond Yale, Jr.,	b. Windham, Ohio, Dec. 11, 1868.
	Los Angeles, Cal.	
1027	Alta C. Yale,	b. " " July 17, 1871.
	Cleveland, O.	
1028 ·	Edith A. Yale,	b. " " Feb. 10, 1874.

1027 Alta C. Yale, m. 1029 Cassius R. Gano, Windham, O., Sept. 26, 1889.
b. Paris, Ohio, Sept. 6, 1867.

(11) C. of 1027 and 1029.

1030	Olive L. Gano,	b. Windham, Ohio, May 2, 1891.
1030²	Clara Edna Gano,	b. Cleveland, Ohio, Aug. 19, 1893.
	Cleveland, O.	

1006 Philip Russell, Jr., m. 1031 Sally E. Jagger, Windham, O., July 4, 1832.
b. Windham, Oct. 5, 1815.
d.   "   April 29, 1877.
m.² 1032 Margaret Owen, Ontario, Can., May 3, 1881.
b. Ont., June 20, 1857 ; d. Ont., May, 1887.

(9) C. of 1006 and 1031.

1033	Sarah Elizabeth Russell,	b. Windham, Ohio, Feb. 12, 1835.
	Windham Ohio.	
1034	Lydia Elmina "	b. " " Jan. 21, 1838.
		d. Newton Falls, Ohio, June 5, 1889.
1035	Alanson R. "	b. Windham, " Jan. 25, 1841.
		d. Newton Falls, " Mar. 19, 1887.
1036	Augusta Lucretia "	b. Windham, " July 28, 1850.
	Windham, Ohio.	
1037	Daniel Jagger "	b. = " " June 8, 1853.
	Helena, Montana.	
1038	Abbie Climena "	b. " " June 13, 1856.

1033 Sarah E. Russell, m. 1039 Joseph Augustus Birchard, Newton, Ohio,
April 19, 1854.
b. Keeseville, Essex Co., N. Y., Apr.6, 1830.

1034 Lydia E. Russell, m. 1040 Henry Butts, Newton Falls, O., Sept. 21,'59.
b. Lordstown, Ohio, Jan. 15, 1825.
d. Newton Falls, Ohio, Feb. 17, 1887. .

(10) C. of 1034 and 1040.

1041 Emerson Elsworth Butts, b. Windham, Ohio, March 21, 1863.

1041 Emerson E. Butts, m. 1042 Ada King, Newton Falls, O., July 15, 1890.

1035 Alanson R. Russell, m. 1042 Mrs. Eliza M. Clark (Johnson).

1036 Augusta L. Russell, m. 1043 Frank Benj. Wolf, Windham, Jan. 1,'83.
b. Hubbard, Ohio, March 11, 1851.

(10) C. of 1036 and 1043.

1044	Nellie Emret Wolf, Windham, O.	b. Windham, Ohio, Nov. 21, 1884.
1045	Abbie Elmina " Windham, O.	b. " " Sept. 12, 1887.
1046	Mary "	b. " " Feb. 10, 1890.

1037 Daniel J. Russell, m. 1047 Amaryllis Rogers, Warren, Ohio, 1874.
b. Vienna, Ohio.

(10) C. of 1037 and 1047.

1048 Bird Carlotta Russell,   b. Geneva, Ashtabula Co., O., May 30, 1875.
Warren, Trumbull Co., Ohio.

1038 Abbie C. Russell, m. 1049 Frank A. Talcott, Ravenna, O., Dec. 29, 1877.
b. Ravenna, Ohio, Oct. 20, 1857.
m.[2] 1050 Frederick Stott, Cleveland, Ohio, 1889.
b. England.

(10) C. of 1038 and 1049.

1051	Carl R. Talcott, Garrettsville, Ohio.	b. Garrettsville, Ohio, Oct. 21, 1879.
1052	Nora Bell Talcott,	b. " " Sept. 15, 1881. d. Cleveland, " Oct. 20, 1881.
1053	Lillian A. " Cleveland, Ohio.	b. " " Oct. 24, 1884.

(10) C. of 1038 and 1050.

1054 Floyd Stott,   b. Cleveland, Ohio, Aug. 15, 1891.

1012 William S. Russell, m. 1055 Emily Irene Merrill, Paris, O., Dec. 24,'48.
b. Braceville, Ohio, July 12, 1823.
d. " " March 28, 1860.
m.[2] 1056 Sarah Jane Oviatt, Braceville, O., July 4, 1860.
b. Braceville, May 10, 1842.

(9) C. of **1012** and **1055.**

1057 Luman Willis Russell, b. Braceville, Ohio, Feb. 28, 1852.
Duke Centre, McKean Co., Pa.
1058 Auren Merrill Russell, b. Braceville, Ohio, Dec. 31, 1857.
d. " " July 13, 1859.

(9) C. of **1012** and **1056.**

1059 Emma Irene Russell, b. Windham, Ohio. May 30, 1862.
Newton Falls, O.
1060 Carlton Andrew " b. " " Feb. 3, 1864.
Newton Falls, O.
1061 Charles Edward " b. " " July 7, 1866.
Newton Falls, O.
1062 Minnie May " b. Paris, " July 2, 1875.
Newton Falls, O.
1063 Vesta Vernet " b. " " Sept. 4, 1877.
Newton Falls, O.

1057 Luman W. Russell, m. 1064 Alice L. Ames, Newton Falls, O., June
18, 1881.
b. Becket, Mass., 1856.

(10) C. of **1057** and **1064.**

1065 Nettie Russell, b. Duke Centre, Pa., April 15, 1883.
Duke Centre, Pa.
1066 Frankie Russell, b. " " June 23, 1885.

1061 Charles · E. Russell, m. 1067 Grace A. P. Thompson, Foxburgh, Pa.,
Jan. 2, 1889.
b. Foxburgh, Pa., 1873.

(10) C. of **1061** and **1067.**

1068 Frank Russell, b. Bradford, Pa., Sept. 30, 1889.
Newton Falls, O.

1013 Daniel A. Russell, m. 1069 Harriet R. Earle, Windham, O., Jan. 1,'57.
b. Windham, Ohio, Oct. 21, 1834.
d. " " April 19, 1859.
m.² 1070 Catharine Murray, Windham, Nov. 20, 1862.
b. Sligo, Ireland, Dec. 28, 1840.

(9) C. of **1013** and **1069.**

1071 Frank Henry Russell, b. Windham, Ohio, March 19, 1859.
U. S. Army, Post Quartermaster, Ft. Barrancas, Fla.

(9) C. of **1013 and 1070.**

1072	Katie May Russell,	b. Windham, Ohio, Aug. 5, 1863.	
		d. Vineland, N. J., Feb. 16, 1883.	
1073	Daniel Abram Russell, Jr.,	b. May's Landing, N. J., May 28, 1867.	
	Vineland, N. Y.		
1074	William Sanford Russell,	b. Vineland, N. J., Dec. 1, 1873.	
		d. " " Jan. 6, 1877.	
1075	Bertha Murray "	b. " " June 12, 1878.	
1076	Maud Sanford "	b. " " May 4, 1882.	
	Vineland, N. J.		

1071 Frank H. Russell, m. 1077 Mary Stuart, Sept. 27, 1884.
b. Millerstown, Pa., May 5, 1865.

(10) C. of **1071 and 1077.**

1078	Julia A. Russell,	b. Fort Wingate, N. M., March 4, 1886.
1079	Mary "	b. Fort Elliott, Texas, Oct. 6, 1890.
1080	Francis "	b. Atlanta, Ga., March 20, 1892.

1073 Daniel A. Russell, Jr., m. 1081 Arabella Kyte, Vineland, Sept. 8, '88.
b. Vineland, March 4, 1870.

(10) C. of **1073 and 1081.**

1082	Edward S. Russell,	b. Vineland, June 20, 1889.
1083	William "	b. " June 3, 1891.

1014 Mary L. Russell, m. 1084 Ira S. Cutts, Windham, O., June 11, 1856.
b. Addison, Vt., Oct. 22, 1829.

(9) C. of **1014 and 1084.**

1085	Pearlea E. Cutts,	b. Paris, Ohio, Nov. 19, 1858.
	Windham, Ohio.	

1085 Pearlea E. Cutts, m. 1086 Charles E. Smith, Windham, Nov. 19, 1878.
b. Windham, June 8, 1857.

1015 Madison J. Russell, m. 1087 Catharine A. Jacoby, Massilon, Ohio,
Dec. 30, 1857.
b. Massilon, Ohio.

(9) C. of **1015 and 1087.**

1088	James M. Russell,	b. Feb. 28, 1860.
1089	Edward "	b. April 25, 1866.

65

1016   Delia E. Russell, m. 1084 Ira S. Cutts, Windham, Aug. 11, 1873.
       b. Addison, Vt., Oct. 22, 1829.

(9) C. of 1016 and 1084.

1090   Daniel I. Cutts,   b. Windham, Ohio, Nov. 24, 1874.
       Windham, Ohio.

1017   Webster B. Russell, m. 1091 Mary Murray, Windham, Dec. 29, 1859.

(9) C. of 1017 and 1091.

1092   Mary C. Russell, who married 1093 Fred. Stevens.

---

  61   Abram Sanford, m. 1094 Clara Howes, Madison, N. Y., April 5, 1820.
       b. Cambridge, N. Y., April 29, 1798.
       d. Hamilton, N. Y., Oct. 5, 1880.

(8) C. of 61 and 1094.

1095   Erastus Sanford,   b. Madison, N. Y., March 5, 1821.
                                d. Elgin, Ill., Aug. 6, 1851.
1096   Martha Amanda Sanford, b. Greene, N. Y., Jan. 6, 1827.
                                d. Hamilton, N. Y., May 4, 1845.
1097   Heman Howes ⌣   "   b. Madison, N. Y., Sept. 29, 1829.
       404 Ostrom Av., Syracuse, N. Y.
1098 , Mary Maria Sanford,   b. Madison, N. Y., Feb. 22, 1836.
                                d. Hamilton, N. Y., June 6, 1855.
1099   William John   "   b. Madison, N. Y., July 27, 1838.
                                d.   "   "   March 30, 1841.

1065   Erastus Sanford, m. 1100 Maria A. Hull, Deerfield, N. Y., Apr. 23, '45.
       b. Wentworth, N. H., Nov. 8, 1817.

1097   Heman H. Sanford, m. 1101 Emily Taylor, Hamilton, June 17, 1857.
       b. Lowville, N. Y., Sept. 13, 1833.

(9) C. of 1097 and 1101.

1102   Alfred Taylor Sanford,   b. Hamilton, N. Y., May 27, 1858.
                                d. Syracuse, N. Y., June 21, 1879.
1103   William John   "   b. Homer, N. Y., Sept. 20, 1861.
       216 Grace St., Syracuse, N. Y.
1104   Clara Daisy Sanford,   b. Homer, N. Y., June 22, 1866.
       404 Ostrom Av., Syracuse, N. Y.
1105   Franklin Taylor Sanford, b. Homer, N. Y., July 9, 1870.
                                d.   "   "   Sept. 23, 1870.

66

1103 William J. Sanford, m. 1106 Alice Livonia Carpenter, Syr., Jan. 1,'90.
                  b. Pompey, N. Y., July 31, 1861.

(10) C. of 1103 and 1106.

1107 Laura Frances Sanford, b. Syracuse, N. Y., July 23, 1891.
1108 Mabel Jean   "   b.   "   "   Oct. 15, 1892.

---

62 Lucretia Sanford, m. 1108[2] David Greenlief, Madison, N. Y.
                  d. Vigo Co., Ind.
            m.[2] 1109 Elijah Hall, Illinois.
Both 62 and 1109 died in Darwin, Ill., about a year after marriage.

(8) C. of 62 and 1108.[2]

1110 William Sanford Greenlief, b. April, 1834.
                  Was in Yuba City, Cal., Jan. 15, 1858.
1111 Janette Greenlief,   b. (?); d. (?).
1112 David   "   b. (?); d. after his mother, about 5 years old.

More complete records of the other members of the families containing the line of our ancestors may be of interest to some. To distinguish these from the family proper the added numbers are followed by the letter a.

46   Joseph Sanford, m. 1 a Ruth ———.

(7) C. of 46 and 1 a.

2 a	Olive Sanford,	b. Aug. 12, 1779.
3 a	William "	b. May 20, 1781.
4 a	Thomas "	b. Dec. 31, 1783.
5 a	John "	b. Nov. 22, 1786.
6 a	Phila "	b. July 9, 1793.

---

48   Peleg Sanford, m. 7 a Lillian, daughter of Cuthbert Wilcox.

(7) C. of 48 and 7 a.

8 a	Samuel Sanford,	b. May 26, 1777.
9 a	Restcome "	b. Sept. 26, 1779.
10 a	Stephen "	b. Oct. 26, 1781.
12 a	Sarah "	b. ——— m. Restcome Hart.
13 a	Lillian "	b. ——— m. Galen (?) Barker.
14 a	Ruth "	b. ——— m. ——— Bosworth.

Samuel (7) 8 a was the father-in-law of Hon. Wm. P. Sheffield, of Newport, R. I.

---

44   Ephraim Sanford had a son Peleg and several daughters.

---

27   Peleg Sanford, m. 15 a Ann D. ——— (?) March 16, 1738.

(5) C. of 27 and 15 a.

16 a	Thomas Sanford,	b. Mar. 12, 1739.
17 a	John "	b. Nov. 21, 1740.
18 a	Philip "	b. Sept. 9, 1743.
19 a	Priscilla "	b. Oct. 2, 1745.

5   Samuel Sanford, m. 20 a Sarah, dr. of William and Mary Wadell, October, 1662.

b. Oct. 1644 , d. Dec. 15, 1680.

m.² 21 a Susanna, dr. of Wm. and Elizabeth Spatchurst, Apr. 13, 1686.

b. ——— ; d. Nov. 13, 1723.

(3) C. of 5 and 20 a.

22 a	Elizabeth Sanford,	b. Oct. 2, 1663.
23 a	John "	b. June 10, 1668.
24 a	Bridget "	b. June 27, 1671.
25 a	Mary "	b. April 27, 1674.
26 a	William "	b. May 21, 1676.
27 a	Samuel "	b. July 14, 1678.

(3) C. of 5 and 21 a.

28 a	Restcome Sanford,	b. Feb. 26, 1687.
29 a	Peleg "	b. Aug. 16, 1688.
30 a	Elisha "	b. Feb. 24, 1690.
31 a	Endcome "	b. Nov. 29, 1691.
32 a	Esbon "	b. Oct. 20, 1693.
33 a	Francis "	b. Oct. 24, 1695.
34 a	Joseph "	b. Aug. 13, 1698.
35 a	Benjamin "	b. June 4, 1700.
36 a	Joshua "	b. April 18, 1702.
37 a	Elizabeth "	b. Dec. 7, 1706.

23 a John Sanford, m. 38 a Frances, dr. of Jeremiah Clark, Sept. 6, 1689.

(4) C. of 23 a and 38 a.

39 a	Samuel Sanford,	b. July 16, 1690.
40 a	John "	b. Feb. 26, 1692.
41 a	William "	b. April 26, 1696.
42 a	Sarah "	b. July 25, 1699.
43 a	Frances "	b. Jan. 12, 1702-3

41 a William Sanford, m. 44 a Experience Bull, July 23, 1717.

b. December 18, 1699.

(5) C. of 41 a and 44 a.

45 a	John Sanford,	b. Feb. 9, 1719.
46 a	William "	b. Oct. 29, 1721.
47 a	Hezekiah "	b. Dec. 29, 1723.
48 a	Elizabeth "	b. Dec. 16, 1725.
49 a	Peleg "	b. June 14, 1728.
50 a	Mary "	b. June 2, 1730.
51 a	Benjamin "	b. Dec. 5, 1732.
52 a	Ann "	b. July 1, 1735.
53 a	Peleg "	b. Sept. 17, 1739.
54 a	Twins "	b. June 28, 1742.

40 a John Sanford, m. 54² a Ann Weedon, (?) Dec. 15, 1713:

(5) C. of 40 a and 54² a.

55 a	Frances Sanford,	b. July 6, 1718.
56 a	Mary "	b. Nov. 22, 1720.
57 a	Ann "	b. Nov. 17, 1722.
58 a	Sarah "	b. Jan. 29, 1725.
59 a	Margaret "	b. July 15, 1727.
60 a	Peleg "	b. Sept. 1, 1729.
61 a	Ruth "	b. Mar. 23, 1732.

26 a William Sanford, m. 62 a Hope, dr. of Geo. Sisson.

(4) C. of 26 a and 62 a.

63 a	Richard Sanford,	b. Mar. 17, 1700.
64 a	Sarah "	b. Oct. 12, 1702.
65 a	Mary "	b. Feb. 16, 1703-4.
66 a	Ruth "	b. Sept. 27, 1706.
67 a	Elizabeth "	b. Aug. 2, 1707.

63 a Richard Sanford, m. 68 a Elizabeth, daughter of John Coggeshall.

(5) C. of 63 a and 68 a.

69 a	William Sanford,	b. Jan. 23, 1723.
70 a	John "	b. June 25, 1725. d, young
71 a	Ruth "	b. Feb. 13, 1728.
72 a	Giles "	b. Feb. 7, 1730.
73 a	Elisha "	b. Nov. 14, 1732.
74 a	Elizabeth "	b. Apr. 13, 1736.
75 a	Sarah "	b. Apr. 10, 1738.
76 a	Peleg "	b. Feb. 28, 1739.

28 a Restcome Sanford, m. 77 a Honora Strange. (?)
      He died at sea 1713.

(4) C. of 28 a and 77 a.

78 a	Samuel Sanford,	b. July 25, 1711.
79 a	Susanna "	b. Jan. 17, 1713.

29 a Peleg Sanford, m. 80 a Sarah, daughter of Josiah Arnold.

(4) C. of 29 a and 80 a.

81 a	Elizabeth Sanford,	b. Sept. 19, 1719. young
82 a	Sarah "	b. July 8, 1724.
83 a	Frances "	May 15, 1726.

30 a Elisha Sanford, m. 84 a Mrs. Rebecca Ware.

(4) C. of 30 a and 84 a.

85 a	Thomas Sanford,	b. Dec. 15, 1715.
86 a	Rebecca "	b. Aug. 29, 1718.
87 a	Joshua "	b. Sept. 2, 1722.
88 a	Frances "	b. Aug. 22, 1724.
89 a	Elisha "	b. Aug. 2, 1726.

32 a   Esbon Sanford, m. 90 a Mary Woodward.

(4) C. of 32 a and 90 a.

91 a	Mary Sanford,	b. 1719.
92 a	Eneas "	b. 1721.
93 a	Woodward "	b. 1723.
94 a	Hannah "	b. 1725.
95 a	Esbon "	b. 1728.
96 a	Benjamin "	b. 1732.
97 a	Lydia "	b. 1735.
98 a	Joshua "	b. 1737.
99 a	Joseph "	b. 1740, (Feb. 18).

99 a   Joseph Sanford, m. 100 a Mary Clarke.

(5) C. of 99 a and 100 a.

101 a	Esbon Sanford,	b. Apr. 7, 1765.
102 a	Peleg "	b. Oct. 18, 1767.
103 a	Joseph "	b. Oct. 25, 1772.
104 a	Mary Ann "	b. Feb. 13, 1775.
105 a	Samuel Clarke Sanford,	b. Dec. 8, 1777. (Drowned at sea).
106 a	Lydia "	b. June 24, 1781.

34 a   Joseph Sanford, m. 107 a Lydia Odlin, (?) Feb. 8, 1721.

(4) C. of 34 a and 107 a.

108 a	Sarah Sanford,	b. Sept. 23, 1723.
109 a	Joseph "	b. —— 24, 1725.
110 a	Daniel "	b. Aug. 5, 1727. (?)
111 a	Martha "	b. July 10, 1732.
112 a	John "	b. 1735.
113 a	Odlin "	b. 1738.

6   Eliphal Sanford, m. 114 a Bartho Stratton.

(3) C. of 6 and 114 a.

115 a	William Stratton.
116 a	Anne "
117 a	Bridget "
118 a	Catharine "

7   Peleg Sanford, m. 119 a Mary (Brenton,) daughter of Wm. and Martha Burton.
   She died 1674.
   m.² 120 a Mary (Coddington,) daughter of Wm. and Ann Brinley.
   b. May 16, 1654, d. March, 1693.

(3) C. of 7 and 119 a.

121 a Ann, m. Capt. John Mason.
122 a Bridget, m. Job Almy, of Tiverton, R. I., Dec. 3 or 6, 1705; d. 1766.
   She had children, Job, Peleg, Mary, Eliphal, Bridget, Ann, John, Deborah.
123 a Elizabeth, m. James Noyes, Sept. 1705.
   A daughter and son.

(3) C. of 7 and 120 a.

124 a   Peleg, b. 1685; d. Boston, 1702, (Stranger's tomb, Kg's Chapel Cemetery.)
125 a   William, b. 1690. Graduate Harvard 1711; d. 1721, (St. Thomas' Cemetery.)

---

125 a   William Sanford, m. 126 a Mrs. Grisselda Sylvester.

(4) C. of 125 a and 126 a.

127 a	Mary Sanford,	b. Dec. 19, 1714.
128 a	Margaret "	b. June 10, 1716.
129 a	Grisselda "	b. June 9, 1720.

---

127 a   Mary, m. 130 a Gov. Thomas Hutchinson, of Mass.

128 a   Margaret, m. 131 a Lieutenant Gov. Andrew Oliver. They went to England with their husbands. Their families settled in England and Nova Scotia.

From other records we learn that 21 Mary, m. Robert Durfee and had children Thomas, John, Benjamin, Peleg, Mary and Elizabeth.

28   Mary Sanford, m. William Brinley, and afterward Josiah Arnold, and had children, Abigail, Josiah, Mary, Content, Catharine and Comfort. She d. July 15, 1721.

Milton Keynes UK
Ingram Content Group UK Ltd.
UKHW020405160124
436085UK00005B/173